HOOSIER PROPHET

Selected Writings of Dan West

HOOSIER PROPHET

Selected Writings of Dan West

Edited by
William Kostlevy and
Jay Wittmeyer

Brethren Press·

Hoosier Prophet: Selected Writings of Dan West
© 2021 Brethren Press

Published by Brethren Press®, 1451 Dundee Avenue, Elgin, IL 60120. For publishing information, visit www.brethrenpress.com.

BRETHREN PRESS is registered in the US Patent and Trademark Office by the Church of the Brethren, 1451 Dundee Avenue, Elgin, IL 60120.

The creation of this book was made possible thanks to financial assistance from the Brethren Historical Library and Archives and Church of the Brethren Global Mission.

Library of Congress Cataloging-in-Publication Data

Names: West, Dan, 1893–1971, author. | Kostlevy, William, 1952– editor. | Wittmeyer, Jay, 1962– editor.
Title: Hoosier prophet : selected writings of Dan West / edited by William Kostlevy, Jay Wittmeyer.
Description: Elgin, Illinois : Brethren Press, [2021] | Includes bibliographical references and index. | Summary: "These selected writings of Dan West (1893–1971) illustrate the influence this visionary Church of the Brethren leader had on peace and service ministries in the twentieth century and beyond"— Provided by publisher.
Identifiers: LCCN 2021015507 | ISBN 9780871783080
Subjects: LCSH: Church work—Church of the Brethren. | Heifer International. | West, Dan, 1893–1971—Influence.
Classification: LCC BX7827.3 .W47 2021 | DDC 286/.5—dc23
LC record available at https://lccn.loc.gov/2021015507

25 24 23 22 21   1 2 3 4 5

Manufactured in the United States of America

For the interns who worked with me at the
Brethren Historical Library and Archives:
Keith Morphew, Andrew Pankratz,
Kelly Brenneman, Aaron Neff, Fred Miller,
Haley Steinhilber, Madeline McKeever,
Zoe Vorndran, and Allison Snyder. —*W. K.*

Which Cross?

Dear Lord, my cross is heavy. The weight of it—
With other things—is bending down my head.
My knees are weak . . . My back and arms are sore.
Do I have to carry it anymore?
Couldn't I just worship yours instead?

Dan West

Messenger, March 16, 1967, 9.

CONTENTS

FOREWORD

When I began work as an intern at the Brethren Historical Library and Archives (BHLA) in 2002, Ken Shaffer, archivist at the time, took me into the back storage room and pointed to a row of filing cabinets and a shelf full of boxes. He then asked if I would be interested in spending my year as intern processing Dan West's papers. They had sat in storage for more than twenty years but had never been fully organized. At first I hesitated, as I stared at the nine filing cabinets and thirty-plus boxes of material, feeling the weight of so much paper and the responsibility for sorting through this man's life and work. But in the end, I agreed and dove right in.

Growing up, I had heard lots of stories about Dan West. We read Mary Garber's *We Raised a Heifer* and supported Heifer Project regularly in my home congregation, my aunts and uncles reminisced about West's visits to their youth camps and Brethren Volunteer Service (BVS) units, and my dad and uncle had taken a cross-country road trip with West in the 1960s. Many Brethren have stories like mine about encounters with Dan West, a man who clearly offered a prophetic voice and vision amid twentieth-century chaos. Sorting, reading, and organizing all of West's papers, I came to realize his vision for the world, his passion for peace, and his concern for the flourishing of all humanity were clear themes throughout his life.

Dan West came by these values honestly. His father, Elder Landon West, wrote a tract celebrating the life of Elder Samuel Weir, the first African American elder among the Brethren. Both family and faith instilled values of racial equity and peace into Dan. Growing up in a small southern Ohio community, and later spending much of his adult life on a farm in Indiana, he also carried a lifelong love for nature and rural communities. These core values are evidenced in this collection, even appearing in his early writings, such as the eulogy to his mother and his concerns around military service in World War I.

The formative experience of West's stay in a military camp—brief though it was—during World War I shaped his consistent call for peace in the world throughout the rest of his life. During the 1930s and 1940s, he worked diligently on peace education among the Brethren by participating in camping programs, drawing on his previous experience as a teacher to focus on children and youth. The selected writings in this book show how he offered suggestions that are still relevant today about how to promote peace teaching in homes and among children. West also worked with several dimensions of the Civilian Public Service program and alternative service for conscientious objectors during World War II and the Korean and Vietnam Wars. He regularly led BVS unit training, offering programs on group dynamics and peace witness for the new volunteers before they headed out to their placements.

Dan West is best known for beginning the Heifer Project, an idea he developed while serving as a relief worker with the American Friends Service Committee during the Spanish Civil War. In the face of malnutrition and starvation in Spain, West saw the rolling hillsides and wondered whether a more sustainable relief path for people—and particularly children—was to provide families and communities with animals that could help them meet basic nutritional needs. His dream became reality through the work of Heifer Project, an organization that quickly extended beyond the Brethren and now helps people the world over stand on their own feet.

West always remained firmly Brethren, or Dunker as he would prefer, despite his engagement with the world. In this collection, you will see his repeated call for Brethren to live up to what he saw as the best of Brethren values—simplicity that avoids affluence, a Brethren approach to peace, a mission of service to the world. Dan West lived most of his life in a period of ongoing war and upheaval on the global stage. Most of these writings were geared to a public and largely Brethren audience, and you will see him wrestle with the state of the world in which drafts, wars, starvation, and growing economic disparities were deep concerns. Throughout his life, West remained skeptical about the role of institution, even though he was employed for many years in denominational roles and became the first layperson chosen as Annual Conference moderator. His repeated calls back to these core values all revolved around a desire to see war cease. Dan West cast a prophetic vision for Brethren and for the world, inviting all to a life of peacemaking, living simply, and caring for the least of these, or "the little people," in his words.

Processing Dan West's papers gave me invaluable insight into the life of this twentieth-century Brethren prophet. In this book, you will catch a glimpse of his passion, his unabashed challenge to consumerism, and his lifelong work in calling for peace. Being around Dan was not always comfortable, because he challenged people to rethink practices and customs, to change their lives, to follow Jesus more closely. As you read, I hope you will feel this same sense of challenge that he extends across time and garner a sense of West's vision for the world.

Denise Kettering-Lane
Associate Professor of Brethren Studies
Bethany Theological Seminary

PREFACE

J uly 14, 2019, marked the seventy-fifth anniversary of the first shipment of animals by the newly established Heifer Project into Puerto Rico, in anticipation of expanding the project into Europe and other parts of a war-torn world. Dan West's big idea of giving families a cow and not a cup would expand from a small, church-based project into a large, value-based nongovernmental organization, Heifer International. In anticipation of the anniversary, as the official Church of the Brethren representative on Heifer's board, I began to pore over the writings of West to find some fresh quotes to use for the occasion and to share with Heifer staff, such as this gem: "Now more than ever before is the time to put our ideals into our practice."

As I read through West's corpus, I began to truly appreciate the breadth of his writings and started to hear a much bigger voice than simply an altruistic call to neighborliness and serviceable citizenship, which is often how he is stereotyped. Dan West really has something to say for the modern reader, or, better said, the post-postmodern reader.

Historically, the Church of the Brethren, to which West belonged, had a strong history of ministry in service "to the glory of God and my neighbor's good." However, the large-scale suffering in Europe beginning with the Great War compelled the church to move beyond its own communities and engage the broader world, fundamentally altering its identity and purpose. It rallied around its proposition that all war is sin. Historian Floyd E. Mallott framed this shift by saying that Brethren service became the third major phase of the church's attempt to present its message to the contemporary world, after Christian tract publication at home and foreign missions abroad.

The church found a call to hands-on ministry—a social gospel—and Dan West was its spokesperson. In the 1940s, the West-inspired Brethren model of systematic, direct people-to-people aid was rare. Today, virtually all religious nonprofit organizations practice it. Episcopalians, Lutherans, and many of the bodies associated with the National Association of Evangelicals, to say nothing of large-scale interdenominational relief organizations like Franklin Graham's Samaritan's Purse, raise money and meet human needs by employing strategies pioneered by the Church of the Brethren seventy-five years ago.

Reading West reminded me of a long-term planning process I participated in as a Heifer board member. Scenario planning, as its name implies, is a management methodology that gives an organization a common framework to understand and strategically address potential outcomes. For example, viewed from the perspective of the subsistence farmer, Heifer developed three scenarios, each centered on the concept of consolidated power. While such farmers were once somewhat immune to outside influence, that environment is dramatically changing. Firstly, megagovernments like China, Russia, and the United States are exerting control and influence far beyond their national borders. Secondly, multinational corporations in such sectors as banking, agribusiness, transportation, and energy, have a major impact on local farmers. Lastly, the newly formed sharing economy, exemplified by Airbnb and Uber, suggests that the nexus of power resides in the hands of smallholding farmers working in solidarity. These individuals connect without mediating agencies, such as governments or multinational corporations.

Dan West persuades with people power. Years before the United Nations, the Marshall Plan, Peace Corps, or the even the Green Revolution, West was working on building a consensus with "the little people" to collaborate and move mountains. West's progressivism is built upon individual sacrifice and communal commitment. He is very wary of the state. In response to Lyndon Johnson's war on poverty, he says: "While the state is promoting a war on poverty, the church might well prosecute a war on affluence. If the two agencies work together honestly, our emerging world in the imminent future might move noticeably toward the kingdom of God."

West does not have a theological voice; he did not lead with his jaw, as he liked to say, but with his hands, contrasting a focus on teaching theology and holding revival meetings to literally building the kingdom of God, one hungry child at a time. He is grateful the Brethren emphasize more than just worship, and even chastises the church community for wasting resources on liturgical and religious trappings.

Heifer International teaches twelve cornerstones to all its group members. Spirituality, the twelfth, manifests itself differently in different contexts, but, for a value-based development agency, a sensitivity to the spiritual is essential. "Passing on the gift" is inherently a spiritual exercise. Many people describe themselves as spiritual, but not religious. This is Dan West. He can work with anyone of any sect or persuasion if there is a shared goal to alleviate suffering. Dan would say this: "We need the help of everyone if we will have peace on earth."

Jay Wittmeyer
Executive Director of Global Mission and Service
Church of the Brethren
2009–20

ACKNOWLEDGMENTS

This collection of Dan West's writings was a joint project of the Brethren Historical Library and Archives (BHLA), Church of the Brethren Global Mission, and Brethren Press. Among the people who worked on this project, several deserve thanks.

Haley Steinhilber created the first working list of possible writings for inclusion. Jessi Marsiglio turned a mass of paper into an editable document, and she and Madeline McKeever proofread everything. James Deaton, managing editor of Brethren Press, shepherded the project.

Previously published content is owned by the Church of the Brethren, except for "Self-Respecting Dunkers," which was originally published in *Brethren Life and Thought*. The rights to West's unpublished materials, including personal correspondences, were given to the BHLA. Great appreciation to the West family for donating these writings for historical preservation.

Editorial note: All of the writings published in this collection have been preserved from the original source material, and only minor corrections, including punctuation, spelling, and capitalization inconsistencies, have been made. Distinctive treatment of words to add emphasis reflects Brethren Press' style guide, which is based on *The Chicago Manual of Style*, 17th ed. In-line [square] brackets denote editorial clarifications.

INTRODUCTION

Members of the Church of the Brethren are frequently asked who and what the Brethren are, and one go-to answer is to say, "We are the people who founded the humanitarian aid organization Heifer International." This answer reveals as much, maybe more, about the people answering the question than it does about the identity of this diverse, complex, and conflicted Protestant church. For to focus denominational identity on fighting hunger and serving those in need is a decidedly mid-twentieth-century emphasis. It is hardly the answer that would have been given by their Dunker ancestors on the American frontier, or even the early twentieth-century Brethren who saddled Dunkers with the unfortunate gendered name of Church of the Brethren.

This book consists of selected essays, letters, and speeches written by one of the principal architects of this mid-twentieth-century Brethren identity—Dan West, the founder of Heifer International. West's vision of building a world without war and hunger sprouts from the very particular soil of the early twentieth-century American Midwest. The vision of a warless world is certainly not unique to the twentieth century, but the distinctive contours of West's concept was shaped by the optimism of early twentieth-century progressivism and its religious arm—the social gospel movement. Emerging out of nineteenth-century evangelicalism, the social gospel applied "the teachings of Jesus and the total message of Christian salvation to society, the economic life, and social institutions . . . as well as to the individual."[1] In short, the church's mission is to embody biblical principles to heal societal ills and effect positive change.

---

1. Shailer Mathews, as quoted in Christopher H. Evans, *The Social Gospel in American Religion: A History* (New York: New York University Press, 2017), 2.

Early Years

Born in 1893, Dan West was the son of German Baptist Brethren, as the Brethren were known before 1908. West's parents, Landon West and Barbara Landis West, were innovative Dunker farmers in Preble County, Ohio. Although Dan never seemed close to his father, in retrospect, it appears they had much in common. Both wrote poetry, taught school, served the church, opposed war, and passionately worked to create a more just social order. Working with older Dunker advocates of racial equality such as Thomas and Sarah Righter Major, Landon West dedicated his life and financial resources to support educational opportunities for Black people and Brethren outreach among them. Landon also wrote a biography of Samuel Weir, the first ordained Black Brethren elder. In his 1909 poem "A Bright Day to Come," Landon West envisioned a future inaugurated by Christ where war would cease and racial harmony would prevail.

Brethren faith and practice shaped Dan West's early life. Dan was baptized in the Sugar Grove, Ohio, congregation in 1904. In his biographical sketch of his mother, found on page 12, Dan celebrates her as a practitioner of such simple Brethren virtues as hard work—living in deeds more than years—and rejection of worldly honor, and recognizes her support of the great cause of her generation, world missions. Working for peace was the great passion of Dan's life, and it presupposed a disciplined faith community deeply rooted in the Scriptures, especially the teachings of the Hebrew prophets and the uncompromising words of Jesus' Sermon on the Mount. With his parents, Dan believed that a bright day was coming and all Christians, but especially Brethren, had a responsibility to help make God's kingdom on earth a reality.

A graduate of Pleasant Hill (Ohio) High School (1911), West attended the Brethren-sponsored Bethany Bible School (1912–13) and Lewis Institute (1913–14), both in Chicago. He received a degree from Manchester College in 1917, and then was drafted into the US Army. West also studied at Columbia University, the University of Chicago, Harvard, and the Ohio State University, and completed all the coursework required for a degree from Cornell University in 1920. He taught industrial arts at Pleasant Hill High School, and in 1923 became principal at Madison High School in Trotwood, Ohio, where he served until 1928.

As a thoughtful young man, West read widely in progressive periodicals such as *The Nation* and other publications influenced by the social gospel like *The Christian Century*, as well as the poetry of Robert Frost and Edna St. Vincent Millay. He was a lifelong collector of quotations, and he sprinkled the wisdom found in these various sources throughout his writings.

Church Leader, Hoosier Farmer

The Church of the Brethren affirmed Dan West's gifts in education and working with youth by calling him to serve. The principal founder of Church of the Brethren youth work in southern Ohio, West, along with Chauncey Shamberger, Joe Van Dyke, Perry Rohrer, and Alvin Brightbill, itinerated across the denomination directing the church's youth program and encouraging young Brethren to study, travel, and receive the training needed to be leaders in their communities. He was appointed to the Church of the Brethren's Board of Christian Education in 1928, and served as Youth Director from 1930–36 and as a staff member in various capacities from 1938–59. In a time of widespread disillusionment with war, West was deeply involved with two important organizational efforts to promote peace teaching in the Church of the Brethren—20,000 Dunkers for Peace and One Hundred Dunkers for Peace. Drawing on Quaker models for peacemaking, West organized Brethren volunteers to work in workcamps and participate in peace caravans. In 1936, he was released from his duties to visit college campuses on behalf of an interdenominational antiwar group, the Emergency Peace Campaign.

In 1932, West married Lucille Sherck. Although a member of the denominational staff for almost thirty years, West chose not to live near the Church of the Brethren headquarters in the Chicago suburbs but instead on farms near Dunlap and Middlebury, Indiana. The Wests were Hoosier farmers, and Dan insisted that he wanted to keep his farm and remain close to the grassroots church. Deeply committed to the Midwestern ideal of farmer families working their own land with minimal hired labor, West looked askance at the growing urbanization of American society and the increasing alienation of individuals and the land that supported them.

Heifer Project

The turning point in Dan West's life came in 1937 during a five-month stint doing relief work in Spain during the Spanish Civil War. Already thinking ahead to the possibility of another world war, West came to believe that the church might develop relief programs as an alternative to military service. Confronting the problem of providing milk for starving children, West conceived the basic ideas that he would develop a few years later into a program initially known as Heifers for Relief. The program received denominational endorsement in 1942, and West's Hoosier neighbors provided the first cattle. In 1944, the first cattle were sent to Puerto Rico. The United Nations Relief and Rehabilitation Agency, with the help of so-called seagoing cowboys who traveled with the cattle, turned a local effort into one of international significance.

By the early 1950s, Heifer Project had become an interfaith venture with ecumenical support. West continued to provide direction as a consultant for many years, until his death. Even after his retirement in 1959, West remained active in peace education, initiated group dynamics programs, and gave direction to Mission Twelve, a Christian education initiative in which small groups from congregations gathered in retreat settings to deepen faith and human relationships and to strengthen the mission of the Church. In 1966, West was elected moderator of the Church of the Brethren Annual Conference, the highest office in the church. At the time of West's death in 1971, Harold Row, director of the Brethren Service Commission, noted that West provided "the ideological base and first practical demonstrations" of the entire denominational program of the church.[2] He was, Row noted, "our architect of brotherhood."[3]

Costly Discipleship

Dan West's prophetic vision received classic expression in a simple poem he wrote late in life that appeared in *Messenger*, the denominational periodical of the Church of the Brethren.

> *Dear Lord, my cross is heavy. The weight of it—*
> *With other things—is bending down my head.*
> *My knees are weak . . . My back and arms are sore.*

---

2. Glee Yoder, *Passing on the Gift: The Story of Dan West* (Elgin, IL: Brethren Press, 1978), 159.

3. Yoder, 159.

Do I have to carry it anymore?
Couldn't I just worship yours instead?[4]

On the surface a critique of a Christianity focused on personal salvation, "Which Cross?" drew its inspiration from a long tradition of Brethren and even non-Brethren evangelically oriented suspicion that mainstream Roman Catholic and Protestant expressions encouraged a morally indifferent "cheap grace." This perspective that celebrated Christian action over God's grace was the subject of critical comment by European Protestant theologians visiting the United States during the era of Prohibition. German Lutherans Dietrich Bonhoeffer and Paul Tillich were both bemused and frustrated by what Bonhoeffer referred to as "Protestantism without Reformation."[5] Tillich placed the blame on European Anabaptist and Pietist immigrants, along with their native Methodist and Congregationalist allies, whose intense moralism had decidedly perfectionistic overtones.[6] After all, even Charles Finney, the famous American evangelist during the Second Great Awakening of the early nineteenth century, had the audacity to argue that the Protestant understanding of salvation by grace through faith undermined holy living and radical Christian social action. For West, like his Brethren forbears, forgiveness was not the point of Jesus' mission but only the beginning of a life of discipleship and Christian service to those in need.

The emphasis on bearing the cross had deep roots in the American Midwest, where the moralism of more recent Scandinavian immigrants mingled with distinct Anabaptist and Pietist traditions and other faith expressions influenced, in part, by Puritan beliefs. West drew deeply on these non-Brethren traditions, including the thought of New England philosopher William James. James' essay "The Moral Equivalent of War" shaped West's lifelong hope to find an alternative to warfare that produced the heroic qualities that many believed were inspired by war. This search for humane pursuits that would instill warrior-like character without mass slaughter inspired some of the most notable humanitarian endeavors of the twentieth century, including the Peace Corps. For Brethren, it inspired both Heifer Project and Brethren Volunteer Service.

---

4. Dan West, "Which Cross?," *Messenger*, March 16, 1967, 9.
5. *Dietrich Bonhoeffer Works*, ed. Clifford J. Green, trans. Douglas W. Stott, vol. 10, *Barcelona, Berlin, New York: 1928–1931* (Minneapolis: Fortress Press, 2008), 305-20.
6. Paul Tillich, *A History of Christian Thought* (New York: Simon & Schuster, 1968), 242.

Social Gospel

A second major influence on Dan West was the human-centered social gospel itself. While his parents drew on the older evangelical activist tradition of the Second Great Awakening and prayed and worked to make the kingdom of heaven a reality on earth, their primary focus remained on the extension of the kingdom through local Christian communities throughout the world. The link between the nineteenth-century evangelicalism of West's parents and the social gospel found clear expression on the mission field and at evangelical colleges in the United States.

Among the most important social gospel influences on Dan West were the writings of Henry Churchill King, president of Oberlin College.[7] The son of an early Oberlin graduate, King spent part of his childhood in Oberlin where his parents, like West's, supported empowering Blacks, worldwide Protestant missions, and temperance. King's central themes included the teachings of Jesus in the Sermon on the Mount, the infinite value of each human being, and the establishment of the kingdom of God on earth. Like West, King dismissed the notion that science and religious faith were mutually exclusive. Scientists dealt with questions of fact; religious faith dealt with the ultimate questions of meaning and destiny. West insisted Brethren use the microscope and the findings of genetics without abandoning the teachings of Jesus.

As West concluded in his influential 1958 essay "The Brethren and the Modern State," found on page 137, it was the duty of Brethren and Christians everywhere to complete the task of turning the "kingdom of the world into the kingdom of our Lord."[8] This inclusive vision, which radically differs from that of early Brethren like Alexander Mack, was deeply rooted in the optimism shared by such classic social gospel writers like King and Walter Rauschenbusch. Like the progressives, but unlike the student radicals of the 1960s and early 1970s, West was comfortable with American and Midwestern democratic traditions. He honored the small town and rural values of fairness, supported the underdog, and directed community-based action to meet human need. Deeply suspicious of large-scale government remedies imposed by outsiders, West supported community-based development models

---

7. West was especially influenced by *Rational Living: Some Practical Inferences from Modern Psychology* (1905). On King, see Donald M. Love, *Henry Churchill King of Oberlin* (New Haven, CT: Yale University Press, 1956).

8. Paul H. Bowman, ed., *The Adventurous Future* (Elgin, IL: Brethren Press, 1959), 131.

based on personal relationships. Heifer Project was just one of the programs established or supported by Brethren who believed that refugee resettlement, international student exchange, and even farmer exchanges could establish the person-to-person relationships that would lay the building blocks for world peace.

In 1971, the year of Dan West's death, Church of the Brethren scholar Dale Brown argued that the doctrine of progress that lay at the heart of the social gospel was the movement's Achilles' heel.[9] For radicals like Brown, the social gospel, shorn of its naïve optimism, remained relevant but needed to honestly acknowledge the reality of human sin even as Christians worked to keep a glimmer of hope alive in a fallen world.

Fifty years later, the concerns of Brethren radicals of the 1960s and 1970s remain relevant. Does the liberal, post-World War II, social gospel-inspired vision of Dan West speak to our own troubled time? Is Dan West's vision too naïve for Brethren and other Christians? The simple answer is no, for West's rejection of materialism and suspicion of large-scale, impersonal institutional solutions to local problems continue to resonate with many around the world. In the essays, letters, and speeches that follow, one finds a vision grounded in the particular soil of the American Midwest that draws on spiritual antecedents reaching back to humble Anabaptist and Pietist immigrants and beyond to Jesus and the Hebrew prophets. In these writings from this Hoosier prophet, one discovers themes and words that echo Jesus' surprising promise that the meek, or "little people," will truly inherit the earth.

William Kostlevy
Director of Brethren Historical and Library and Archives
Church of the Brethren
2013–21

---

9. Dale W. Brown, *The Christian Revolutionary* (Grand Rapids: Eerdmans, 1971), 83-102.

1.

FORMATION
OF A PROPHET

An understanding of Dan West begins with the Church of the Brethren's vacillating response to World War I. The Great War demonstrated that Brethren were no longer a people set apart, and that modern warfare made even nonresistant Christians part of the military machine. The confused Brethren response to conscription, the purchasing of war bonds, and the military itself is reflected in a letter West wrote to William J. Swigart, secretary of the church's Central Service Committee. While West's papers do not include Swigart's response, we do know the Central Service Committee, appointed by the special Goshen Conference in 1918, encouraged drafted Brethren to accept noncombatant service under military direction. This position would prove unacceptable to church leaders later, leading Brethren to join Friends and Mennonites in the organization of Civilian Public Service as the preferred Brethren option during World War II.

The reflection West wrote for his mother, following her death in January 1933, beautifully captures the love and respect of a son for his mother. It also gives insight into the values most admired by this champion of humanitarian aid. The opening clause of this tribute, "if we live in deeds more than in years," summarizes a central emphasis of West's theology.

West's 1925 commencement address to the graduates of Newton Township High School in Pleasant Hill, Ohio, suggests that West's mature emphasis on world citizenship instead of an ethnocentric nationalism is present long before his exposure to human suffering during the Spanish Civil War.

A list from a letter West wrote to his friend and coworker Joe Van Dyke in 1928 captures West's belief that Judaism and Christianity provide the key to understanding life's meaningfulness. This conviction would remain as he tackled issues of war, poverty, and social injustice throughout his life.

Letter to William J. Swigart

Pleasant Hill, Ohio
April the Fifteenth
1918

Dear Brother Swigart,

As I am very likely in the next draft to be called, April 26, there are some questions I should like to have answered, if you can tell me:

1. Will the noncombatants be asked to bear arms in the departments the president has declared noncombatant?

2. Is there any opening for the enlistment of noncombatants in civilian service?

3. Is there any possibility of enlistment of noncombatants in noncombat service? And if so, is it desirable?

4. Can a noncombatant not yet drafted apply for special agricultural service? If so, how?

5. From the standpoint of our peace principles, which of the branches of service declared noncombatant is most constructive and most in harmony with them? Or is there no appreciable difference?

6. Is it wisdom to accept the uniform?

7. Is form 1008 sufficient to take along to camp?

I thank you.

Your brother,
Daniel West

Dan West to William J. Swigart, April 15, 1918, box 3, William J. Swigart Papers, Brethren Historical Library and Archives.

Mother

If we live in deeds more than in years, mother lived more than seventy-eight years, seven months, and twenty-six days. She was born June 2, 1854, in Darke County, Ohio, the third of fourteen children in the family of Daniel and Susanna Landis. Most of her first twenty years were spent in Darke County. The chills and fever of malaria and the remedies they used made her youth not too pleasant. She was delicate and the family physician said that Barbara would never live long.

The next eight years she lived as hired girl with Uncle John and Aunt Christena Miller. From their home she went Oct. 18, 1882, as the wife of Elder Landon West to Adams County.

The next spring they moved to Preble County. There they lived and toiled for the next seventeen years and there all of the children were born. Mother carried the burden alone when father was away preaching. Sometimes she paid his expenses out of her hard-earned money.

In 1900 mother purchased her father's farm and there she labored for twenty years more. Father passed away in 1916; mother carried that sorrow graciously. In 1920 a severe attack of pneumonia weakened her permanently. The lifetime habits of toil and the eagerness to be busy at worthwhile things, drove her on, but her old-time endurance was gone. It was deeply disappointing to her that she could no longer do things when she had the will to do them.

In November 1932, her heart weakened and it never recovered. On Saturday morning, Jan. 28, 1933, she passed as she had lived, quietly.

She leavers four sisters and one brother, three stepchildren, five children, eleven grandchildren, and two great-grandchildren.

She was a pioneer mother, accepting hardship as the common lot, and seemingly tireless in middle-life, she worked eighteen and twenty hours out of twenty-four regularly. Her hands have turned the spinning wheel; they have broken flax and carded wool; they have plied the knitting and the sewing needle. They did all the duties that make up the regular part of woman's work. They have also grubbed new ground, wielded the pitchfork and corn cutter,

---

Dan West, "Mother," *Gospel Messenger*, March 18, 1933, 27, 30.

built stone fences of boulders as a part of man's work. They have done all that goes with farm work except plowing.

She was eager for knowledge. In her youth it wasn't customary for girls to have much schooling and delicate health prevented her going beyond the fifth reader, but she wanted to learn. She liked geography and enjoyed hearing of travel. Too busy to read much in her active life, she spent hours with her Bible in her latter years. She borrowed money for higher education even when it was not for her own flesh and blood. She learned the fundamentals of life. The best university professors are now teaching the values she taught in her own way.

She loved righteousness. She stood for it steadily and spoke plainly when words were needed. Injustice in the community and crime news in the papers hurt her deeply. She rejoiced in the truth.

Timid and shy as a girl, she learned to love and trust people—old folks, young people, and children, and she was glad for honest visitors. Young people liked to talk to her.

She was sensitive to beauty and order even when she could not always have them. She hated weeds. It was simple art that drew her—flowers, quilts, homely jokes, simple poems, and old hymns. Often she sang at her work.

Her religion dealt largely with actual living. It was not merely a waiting for the next world: It was loving God with the whole heart and one's neighbor as one's self. She lived and taught forgiveness. She had no use for emotional religion. She was baptized near Sugar Grove at the age of twenty-one, after a regular church service.

Last fall she said that she was not afraid of death and she put great faith in the resurrection. Her faith in God gave her a quiet endurance in a world of toil and change.

She struggled against poverty most of her life, but she taught continually against the love of money. She gave more freely than she spent money for herself. She liked to read the story of Paul, the first foreign missionary and soldier of the cross. She gave gladly to missions. She requested that no flowers be used at her funeral, but that any wanting to give flowers should give the money to missions instead.

These are some of the facts. She did not care for praise and would not have it here. Words are not adequate anyhow, only the carrying on of the things she lived for will be a just tribute to mother.

Commencement Address to Newton Township High School

Mr. Chairman, Neighbors and Friends, and Graduates of 1925:

I am happy to be here tonight. I am always glad to come back to my home community, and especially at times like this. The last time I spoke to this class, it was under quite different circumstances. There were no flowers, no graduating clothes, no diplomas in sight; and there was no crowd looking on. But the work we did together stands out rather clearly in my mind. And I feel particularly honored in the privilege of speaking to a class I once taught—on the last night of their public school life.

It may be that I did not do a very good job of teaching you, two years ago, and you may have invited me back to one last chance to make things right. All right, I'll do my best to square up a year's work in forty or forty-five minutes.

I believe your examinations are taken, your grades made out, and your diplomas signed and ready for you. But I should like to ask for the permission to give the final examination, as soon as I get through with my speech.

- - - - -

About 120 years ago one of my great-grandfathers secured a deed for some government land, and settled in the woods, north of town. And the great-grandfathers of many of you did likewise, here in Newton Township, or elsewhere in the Miami Valley.

They had come to establish homes for themselves and their families in the new state. They toiled to clear the land, and to raise their crops. If you have ever grubbed out one stump you have a small sample of their regular work for a large part of the year. They endured privations, hardships, and much sickness. They lived and died—many were short lives—and they lie buried in the six or more graveyards in the township, or in the private burying grounds, many of which are now forgotten.

Dan West to Newton Township (Ohio) High School, 1925, box 24, Dan West Papers, Brethren Historical Library and Archives.

There was once a corduroy road where we have now a concrete pike. They had swamps where we have farms. At one time, they tell me, a man living on the Troy Pike would sometimes come in a canoe as far as the Hixson Farm, and then walk into Pleasant Hill. They had no radios, no railroads, no interurban lines, no automobiles, no telephones, no electric light, no store clothes, no funny papers—they did not have much of anything as we sometimes look at it.

But they did have a purpose, a faith, and a determination. They established churches—the first one, over a hundred year ago. They established schools, in log houses at first; then a later generation built the little red schoolhouses, each the best in their day. A good many of us know pretty well the old building that used to stand out in front of this one. Now we have this large plant, as evidence of our best.

Many of the earlier pioneers had no schooling; some could not write their own names. Some had a few months, some a few years; and a generation ago a few were able to finish the high school work. But I doubt if the parents of one-third of the class ever had the chance to finish high school; they had to work instead.

Does that mean anything to you? Your twelve-year opportunity of public schooling is from one and a half to two times as much as your parents had; three or four times what your grandparents had, and from six to twenty or more times what your great-grandparents had. I don't think I have overestimated here, in most cases. These generations have lived and toiled and sacrificed in order that you might have what you enjoy tonight. They have invested in you; and I think it is a good investment. I hope they will never regret it.

What we have—speaking generally—they gave us; what we are, they made us. And yet we seem inclined to forget that we are a product of that pioneer life. It is so far away and long ago that it does not seem important. But I think we should stop occasionally and look back that we might better understand our heritage; and I think the more we know of our forefathers, the better we shall appreciate them. If we expect to do as well with our opportunity as they did with theirs, we have put a hard task before us.

- - - - -

There is another side to the picture. Our forefathers were not perfect—they did not claim to be. And I know we are not perfect. Because it is always easier to see people's faults than their good qualities, let us be careful and charitable. But let us look at the other side a bit.

Our forefathers left us a good deal of unfinished business—and some hard problems.

They did not always manage their farms as wisely as they might have done; and today many farms will not produce the crops which they produced one hundred years ago. I am told that some farms in France are more fertile now than they were one thousand years ago, and they have been farmed constantly. Our forefathers did not always study markets—their business was to produce. They did not always look ahead; they did not always buy and sell wisely. They allowed other people to take advantage of them, not once or twice, but many times. Sometimes they took advantage of each other. There are other causes, but that problem is certainly here. Right now the parents and relatives of some of you are anxious about the outcome of their business. You likely do not know what they have given up in order that you might come to where you are tonight. You people have inherited the problem of how to make a comfortable living.

Another problem—that of keeping up with other folks. It shows sometimes in graduating dresses. One girl gets a high-priced dress; at once another feels that she must have one just as costly—preferably a little more costly. That grows until it has put a hardship on the parents of the whole bunch. And the girls don't know more because of it; sometimes they don't look any better; and I am sure they don't like each other any better because of it.

It is much the same with the boys. One boy's dad is foolish enough to get a new car for him to use; immediately other boys feel the need of one just as high-powered and as high-priced.

Sometimes the older folks get bitten by the same bug. The neighbors have bought a new rug, or a new set of silverware. And here is the argument: "We have got to have one just as good; we're just as good as they are."

Again, one man builds a house—a fine one. That is the hint for another to match him, or "do a little better."

I don't know whether the fur coat business has struck Pleasant Hill yet, or not. It has hit some places pretty hard. They are still wearing them in Hammond. Yes, it has been hot there, but that does not make the difference. And fur coats are costly, but that isn't the point. A good many folks there have to keep up with other people.

It is a poor game—for everybody loses, except the ones that sell the luxuries. It is an absurd game, for it takes money from the things of greater worth, and gives it to the things of less worth. Economists call it the standard of living. It makes the problem of making a living much harder than it would need to be. Our forefathers, good as they were, did not teach us that it does not take a fortune for one to be happy and helpful. Maybe they tried, because I think many of them knew it, but we would not learn. Anyhow we have that problem, too.

There is a third problem. Our forefathers did not leave us a perfect community. Some people still envy others; some still gossip about their neighbors; some hold spite and bitterness, some betray the confidence that others have in them; some live on a pretty low plane of character. It is still easy for some boys and girls to go wrong in this community—and some men and women, too.

Our forefathers with the forefathers of other communities left us another problem—and a big one: How to get along with our neighbors—other nations, I mean.

The spirit of comradeship between the Allied nations during the [Great] War was going to last, we were told. But it has not lasted. Some in America are jealous of Britain; some are distrustful of France; some are hating Japan just as heartily as they once hated Germany. And I suppose there are people in every one of these countries who feel all three ways about America.

It has been estimated that the countries of the earth were eleven times nearer each other in 1914 than they were one hundred years before—in terms of transportation. So long as your neighbor is eleven miles away, you can think what you please about him, and say it, and do what you please; and it won't make much difference. But let him move up within one mile; and then you can't say and do just what you please without getting into trouble.

Several weeks ago I was talking with a man in Hammond about the naval maneuver in the Hawaiian Islands. I asked him what he thought the effect would be on Japan. He said he didn't think she would do anything, whatever way she felt about it. He went on to say that we will have to fight Japan someday anyhow, and that we might as well get ready for it. I asked him what we would fight about, and although he did not give any reasons, he seemed to feel strongly that we had to do it.

A week ago last Saturday night, I was privileged to sit in a conference of university students at the University of Chicago where some of the problems of the Pacific were being discussed. One was the naval maneuvers. The majority of students there, from eight or more different countries, voted that such movements were offensive (not defensive) and that they did not tend toward the preservation of peace.

Last year I read of a man in Oklahoma, who saw one evening another man walking slowly down the road in front of the house. Neither had ever seen the other before. The owner of the farm went out and ordered the man to move on. This man wasn't inclined to take orders from a stranger, and refused. The owner came into the house, told his wife that he didn't like the looks of the fellow, got his gun, and went out to drive him away. They argued a bit, then exchanged several shots. When the shooting was over, both men were dead. Probably each one thought that he was defending his rights. What either one gained wasn't much.

Unless we learn somehow to get along with our neighbors, many statesmen are telling us, we won't have any neighbors, because they won't be here, and we won't be here, either.

There are other problems, but these four are hard enough:
a. how to make a comfortable living.
b. keeping up with other people.
c. community life, and
d. how to live in peace with other nations.

Any of them are big enough for you to tackle. Unless you do tackle them, they are bound to be harder for the next generation.

These are some of the unfinished things that our forefathers have left us. Let [us] remember again, it is easier to criticize than to do something constructive; and let us also remember that the faults of our forefathers were the faults of not knowing, rather than the faults of wrong purpose. We who have had a chance to know more, can do more if our purpose is as high as that of many of our forefathers.

(You are not forgetting about that examination, I hope.)

Perhaps some of you are wondering why I am not telling a bunch of funny stories. At commencement time I don't feel exactly funny. Perhaps others are wondering why I have been talking of these hard problems, when I might be telling you how good-looking you are, how intelligent you are, and how proud we should be of you, and when I might be painting rosy pictures of what you will do in the world.

It is a good-looking bunch—take them as a bunch that way. And I know you have good gray matter—I have dealt with it. And I am proud of you. But I am not sure about the rosy picture. It all depends.

Let me tell you what some high school graduates have done. They got away from home as soon as they could, cut loose from any obligation to their community and its problems, and their idea seems to have been: "to get theirs while the getting was good." Some became wealthy, some famous. But not many of them took their share of the responsibility for the problems they inherited. That is one reason why the problems are so hard now.

You can help if you want to help; but you are not compelled to help. Responsibility is always taken, not given. I hope you take your share, and do the best you can with it.

Some people—well-informed people, too—are frankly gloomy about all four of these problems. I am not, if we are willing to fulfill three requirements: intelligence (all you've got), the spirit of the Christ, and hard work and cooperation.

Four of you are going to college, I am told; five to normal [schools], three to business school, six to the farm or shop, one to nursing, and one will stay at home. These are all fields of possible happiness and service. Several of you are undecided. There is no rush, if you take the first opportunity, and strive to find the field of work that calls out the best in you.

But whatever you do, and wherever you go, I hope you remember these four problems: how to make a comfortable living (not just you, but other people at the same time), the matter of keeping up with other folks, the problem of community life, and the problem of world peace. Somebody has to work on them if they are ever to be settled.

- - - - -

Now for the examination questions. Some are hard ones; but you see, I don't mind asking hard questions. I have tried to get important questions, which can't be answered out of a book. I should like to have you try them now, and then lay them away until about June 1, and then try them again.

The Final Examination

1. Do you have a big purpose for which to live?

2. Are you willing to earn your happiness and freedom?

3. Are you still willing to learn?

4. Can you face realities? Are you honest with yourself?

5. Do you have the habit of give-and-take?

6. Can you produce an honest day's work? Are you afraid of hard work?

7. Can you be happy doing without things that other people have?

8. What are the names of your friends? Would you like to have your mother know them as well as you know them?

9. Will the girls (boys) who know you have a better regard for boy (girls) because they have known you?

10. Which way are you looking, toward Pola Negri and Jack Dempsey, or toward the Master?

11. Will the life you are planning be a carrying on of the best in your home, and the best in your community?

12. Are you ambitious to become a World Citizen, as well as a Citizen of America?

13. Do you want to "Be Something," or do you want to "Do Something"?

14. Can you build tomorrow on what you have done today and yesterday?

15. Do you expect to find that your school days were your best days?

Now let us think about that rosy picture again. If you can honestly answer these questions in one way, I can't make it too rosy. If in another, I can't make it quite so rosy. If in still another, I should have to paint a pretty dull and drab picture. You see why I can't be sure about it.

This is a rough world. The glory of commencement does not wear well for more than a week or so, except in the memory. And I should like to help you preserve some of the values of this high moment for you. Tonight you are here, your high school work in the past, your diplomas ready, your classmates all together, your parents here before you, your friends and neighbors gathered here to honor you on the last night of public school life.

And here I am, trying to help you appreciate a little more the struggle and sacrifice that has given you what you have, and trying to point out some of the unfinished problems which you ought to help solve.

Now look ahead. Next week, gingham aprons, overalls, dishwater, disc harrows, spades and shovels, chores. Did you ever stop to think that a hungry pig has no respect whatever for a high school diploma? These words represent the work of this summer for many of you—and it has to be done. A few of you may think it well enough that our forefathers did all hard unpleasant labor, but that we won't need to do anything like that. I hope you are not so ungrateful.

One of the purposes of a high school education, I think, is to grasp some of the finer things of life, and bring them down to the common tasks, and so to make them full of meaning and intelligent and beautiful service.

I am mentioning some of these common things now, when the best things seem possible to you, in order that when you get back to those common tasks, you will remember to hold the high resolution you have tonight.

In closing I want to repeat that I am happy to be here. My commencement wish for you is the faith that was Browning's: [quote is missing].

A Cross Section of What I Believe

Spring 1928

1. I believe in laws (probable sequences): physical, chemical, biological, psychological, spiritual. I cannot draw sharp lines between those fields; however, [Henry] Drummond says the same laws operate in the natural and spiritual worlds. He is helpful to me (*Natural Law in the Spiritual World*).

2. I believe in afterthoughts. History is a part of them. Shailer Mathews says we get the idea of direction of a ship's course from the wake in the water; so with the idea of human progress, we infer it from the "wake" of history.

3. I believe in intelligence: the placing of worthy goals, the adapting of means to reach them, and self-criticism. I believe that the best ways of living can endure the light of rational criticism.

4. I believe in goodness, the kind of action and attitude that abides, that can be built upon. "The bad man annuls today what he did yesterday. The good man builds today upon what he did yesterday" [William Torrey] Harris.

5. I believe in friendship, the integrating of spirit of several persons, to their mutual helpfulness and lasting happiness.

6. I believe in sacrifice as investment and net gain, not net loss—water on higher levels because it was not allowed to leak out in the basement.

7. I believe in evolution as the process God is still using in guiding the universe, and the process used by good men and women, the process at work in all religions, and culminating in the life of the Master. "The goal of evolution is Jesus Christ." [Henry] Drummond. Donald Hankey's *Religion and Common Sense* is good. As to the evolution of one's own faith, here is a good phrase from Tennyson—"faith that comes of self-control."

Dan West to Joe Van Dyke, spring 1928, box 1, Joe Van Dyke Papers, Brethren Historical Library and Archives.

8. I believe that the Power back of the universe is not aimless, not self-destructive, not opposed to personal values, but going somewhere, "kind in His justice," and at least as much as personal, perhaps much more. It is a great synthesis in one word—God. Only Judaism and Christianity have made that great generalization.

9. I believe in the "more abundant life," to give which to other people was the big drive back of the Master's life—a cyclical integration of the most honest thought, and the widest knowledge, and the best choices in living into a continually increasing happiness and helpfulness—so that anytime we may pause to look up from work, and think a bit, we can strike a balance, and say sincerely that life is good, and that it promises even greater good. I don't need to say that I *believe* this—I know it.

D. W.

II.

CHRISTIAN HUMILITY

⸻

Throughout his life, Dan West was suspicious of religious and academic titles and even human recognition.

West reflects on his decision to reject the offer to accept an honorary doctorate from his alma mater, Manchester College, now University, in this 1966 letter to President Blair Helman.

In the second document, West acknowledges that, like all of us, he could have done more to prevent war and injustice in his lifetime, and that all humans share in this guilt.

⸻

Letter to Blair Helman

407 Marilyn Avenue, Goshen, Ind.
14 May 1966

A. Blair Helman
Manchester College

Dear Blair,

Your second invitation for me to accept an honorary degree from Manchester has returned to my thinking several times since you telephoned me nearly two weeks ago. Never having tried to make my reasoning on this matter articulate, this will not be an adequate explanation. But it is my best so far.

Many memories come back in this connection. Here are some that seem important:

1. From both parents I came to prefer the little people of the earth.

2. At Lewis Institute in Chicago (1914–15) my imagination was caught by Prof. E. H. Lewis (no relative of the founder) in literature and philosophy. And something stuck in my mind when he said to the class one day, "I have four doctor's degrees I will sell cheap. Do you know I am a doctor of laws? But I don't know what laws should be passed for street cleaners."

[number 3 is missing]

4. When I graduated from Manchester (1917) I felt more ignorant than ever before—was a little reluctant to take the AB degree.

5. My half brother (medical doctor) P. C. West said in the 1920s, "You won't know any more with a doctor's degree, but it will add $1500 to your salary."

6. At Columbia University (1919) Prof. O. W. Caldwell was a brilliant science teacher but his humor transcended his scholarship.

Dan West to Blair Helman, May 14, 1966, box 15, Dan West Papers, Brethren Historical Library and Archives.

7. At Ohio State University (summers 1922–23) Prof. B. H. Bode (I was told the highest paid faculty member there) stretched my horizon on the relativity of intelligence and some other things. But he was disappointing in private on his sense of responsibility.

8. At Cornell University (1923–24) Dr. Theodore Eaton seemed to brag about his ignorance just before he spotted ours. One of the best teachers I ever had, he liked common people, even though he urged me to get ready to work with graduate students.

9. Also at Cornell (same year) Dr. E. L. Palmer [opened] fields of interest in nature study. On a field trip one day we passed by a certain telephone pole. Stopping us he said that is where he took his PhD degree. Then he explained: "When I took my AB degree here I thought it was something big. But when I took my AM degree, it did not seem very important. When I took my PhD degree I didn't care to attend the ceremony, but they had a ruling that if one were in town he must attend it. This telephone pole is just outside the city limits."

10. Opportunities to take graduate work at Columbia and Yale did not pull me as hard as the chance to work with the people in rural communities. For a long time I have tried to be versatile, and I still like to keep in touch with the greatest minds I can get to know in every country. However I want to have no great gap between me and the common people. One can learn much of importance from both.

Working with them, especially youth, has been fun for many years—until somebody puts me on a pedestal—an uncomfortable place. Then I slide down as fast as I can where there is more real freedom. And it seems to fit better with brotherhood.

These words from James Quinter, perhaps a century ago, are valid for me now: "If you are a worthy member of the family of Christ . . . worthy of the name 'Christian' . . . there is more in that name than in all the honorable titles which the world can heap upon you."

Again I want to thank you for your kindness in offering a second chance for an honorary degree. And the chance to get it with Norman Cousins pulls also. But the two pulls at the same time are not strong enough yet.

Meantime I want to keep on learning as much as I can digest and share for another ten years—if possible—with you and other great spirits whose deep aim is responsible education in a changing world.

Gratefully yours,
Dan West

We Criminals

Maybe you don't like this title. Well, I don't either. Let's look at the meaning further.

Some years ago in a courtroom in Nuremberg, Germany, I sat on the same bench where Hermann Goering had sat. I didn't sit at the same prisoner's desk where he had pleaded for his life along with some twenty-eight other war criminals—but lost his case. He was convicted of war crimes and condemned to death along with some twenty others. The rest of those were hanged and their bodies burned and their ashes scattered but he "cheated the gallows"—by taking poison before they got to hang him.

Never guilty of any of the crimes that he committed and so far having tangled with the law only by overparking and running a traffic light that changed too fast—in that now quiet room in Nuremberg I felt something akin to being in a real sense guilty of the crime of war. Yes, I can assure you that I have done *something* for peace beginning not long after I was honorably discharged from the United States Army in 1919. Some kind people have said that I have done considerable for peace—maybe more than they expected of me, and some others have been generous in their compliments, but all of this does not release me from this feeling of guilt—the crime, negligence.

Not so conceited that I believe my efforts could have prevented World War II or the Korean War or the war in Palestine or the Congo or Vietnam, or could have persuaded Harry Truman not to drop the first atom bombs on Hiroshima and Nagasaki (I was utterly ignorant of them then). My crime consists in not doing all that I could have done, [but] allowing for the many things I could not have done, I could have been one of a few thousand or a few hundred thousand as determined as were the makers of the atom bomb in antidoting the forces leading to war. This is the reason for the title "We Criminals," are you with me?

From the perspective of many years I see a number of things that I could have done, felt some of them then but did not do much of anything about them:

Dan West, undated, box 49, Dan West Papers, Brethren Historical Library and Archives.

1. In the late 1920s when Gustav Stresemann pleaded at Geneva with the [League of Nations] to give credit and he could save democracy for Germany. Some supposedly responsible people laughed at him. My beloved America was not then a member of any such organization but could have spoken and I might have helped to work in that direction. I didn't.

2. When the [Kellogg-Briand] Pact was signed in Paris (I was one of the few thousand standing outside the Quai d'Orsay while it was being signed) I could have begun working with representatives and senators in America to act as though we believed that true. Single-handed I could not have done much but a few thousand or hundred thousand might have tipped the scale in the 1930s.

3. When Hitler had his army march into the Rhineland I remember well that Sunday morning. I did a little something about it, I talked to two persons, gave them my feeling of the seriousness of the situation, but that's about all I did.

4. When in 1937 Franklin Roosevelt at Chicago gave his speech on quarantining the aggressors I was told this built two Japanese battle ships. I did nothing about that.

5. In 1938 in London in his office George Lansbury told me of his pilgrimage to the heads of government of fourteen countries trying to change their minds. I was impressed by this. He said that Hitler was very friendly, gave him two hours, complained that nobody trusted him. This impressed me. I was in no position to do anything like that, but suppose I had picked up that cue and kept working ever since, maybe I could have been influential someplace in heading off later wars. I did nothing.

6. In 1940 I helped to establish Civilian Public Service and worked in awkward ways to try to make that a real peace witness, but I could have done more.

7. In 1941 I knew about the efforts of [Toyohiko] Kagawa in Japan and [E.] Stanley Jones in America to try to head off the coming war. All I did was to pray for them and talk a little.

8. After [Representative] Jeannette Rankin had voted against entering the war with Japan, the day after Pearl Harbor, I could have supported her better. My congressman told me the story of talking with her just after the vote. I did nothing about it.

9. In 1942 (I believe) when H. G. Wells wrote "Berlin Should Be Bombed" I felt that he was doing wrong, but I did nothing about it.

I could go on at greater length, but maybe I have made my case. I am guilty of the crime of neglect. Are you too?

Some weeks ago a regular series on TV from University of Michigan dealt with educational programs for ordinary listeners and the legal aspects of negligence were featured on one of those programs. An incidence was reported. An airplane dropped into a man's field and did damage to his crops, but the pilot doing all he could was not held finally responsible because he had a defective motor. In the court case they traced the cause back to the manufacturer and even to the maker of the steel that went into the motor and somebody there was held responsible.

The speaker insisted that nobody is entitled to the protection of the law when he does something wrong, even if ignorantly, and he believes this may be the wave of the future. This quote is worth giving, "The law is trying to keep pace with modern science and technology."

If this is true in regard to protecting human life from accident in the retail aspect of life, how much more true and how much more responsible I ought to be—you too if you like—for the forces that may destroy all of human life in the wholesale. Here is where "we criminals" might well get oriented to the future and get busier than we've ever been.

Back in 1928 in Geneva, Switzerland, Professor John [Maynard Keynes] of Cambridge University, England, spoke to a handful in an education seminar there. Among other things he said, "It is your business to create the spiritual stuff out of which international law is made."

In 1946 Archibald MacLeish wrote, "We now accept the miracle of the atom but we do not yet accept the miracle of the human heart." This stuck in my mind and when I had opportunity I reminded him of this and asked what he meant. He said he did not know but encouraged me to learn what I could and come back and tell him. Apparently this job of preventing war and establishing peace is a much more complex and delicate and difficult task than even the creation of an atom bomb. If so, those of us who believe it are wise to get busy trying, ignorant as we are, to find the formula and apply it. That is if we are not to be guilty of further criminal neglect.

This is no matter of real discouragement but just sober responsibility. James Bright, the old friend of American democracy, said one time, "Minorities always control whatever form of government you have." We have seen that sort of thing happen in negative ways, for example, a handful of I believe only seven persons in a beer cellar in Munich some forty years ago. They set the pattern for the Nazi epidemic over Germany. Could a highly responsible, but determined, group set the pattern for the future? Beginning as ignorant and awkward as we are, I am betting that it is not impossible.

Looking at it from 1965 on it may be only a few minutes to midnight as they say in the bulletin of atomic scientists. Maybe before 1970 some of these many atom bombs will go off, either by intent or by accident, as C. P. Snow has predicted. In case that should happen the whole human race may be destroyed as Otto Hahn told me only five years ago. But I hold that as long as there is life there is hope. Maybe it is not too late to work unless we do too little.

Give me another ten years to work with the help of a handful of people, some pacifists, some not pacifists, but all determined to work against war and for peace, maybe we can help to a difference. My own emphasis ought to be more positive than negative. This is why I want to work on the Heifer Project as well and as long as I can. But the minor needs to be negative also. Here the writers of the article "The Test Ban" in *Scientific American* for October ought to have a great deal of support and so ought everybody else going our way. I am very sober but I am hopeful that within two years from now there will develop a handful of determined, if ignorant, people who will work together to help make possible a world outgrowing war, striving towards peace. That will be the great world society.

III.

AUTHENTIC WORSHIP

D**an West was a** lifelong critic of conventional Christian worship. His suspicion of religious symbolism and vocabulary is captured in this 1945 letter to fellow peace advocate Rufus Bowman, then president of Bethany Biblical Seminary. For West, Bethany's decision to raise funds and build a chapel, complete with stained glass windows and other trappings of modern church architecture, violated Brethren tradition and human need, given the great suffering after World War II. The chapel's term of service was cut short, although the stained glass windows still exist at the current Bethany Theological Seminary campus in Richmond, Indiana.

In the *Messenger* editorial written as moderator, West praises Brethren for emphasizing doing more than worshiping.

In the third document, West considers attempts to tie God's presence to holy places. West believed that faithful and unelaborate worship in simple meetinghouses was vital not only for Brethren but for all followers of Christ. Authentic worship is also centered on following Christ and keeping his commandments. As West writes, "Jesus never asked anybody to understand him or to worship him. But he did ask some to follow him, including us."

Letter to Rufus Bowman

Rufus Bowman
3435 W. Van Buren St.
Chicago 24, Ill.

Dear Rufus:

Thank you for your letter of August 1 about the chapel. I had heard about it but was not present when the item was presented to the Council of Boards. I have done some thinking about it and want to pass on my "thinks" for your consideration and my further information.

1. Whether. This may be an unkind question to raise but I think you will appreciate it from my standpoint. I think it is about thirty-three years since I first went to Bethany. It was a little place then and quite different from what you have now. We worshiped over in Building A, in rooms now occupied by the first-floor apartments. It was crowded, it was not aesthetic nor even convenient, but we worshiped. Later, I remember the pounding radiators and creaky floors over in the old chapel in Building B, and I resented somewhat those heavy pillars in the way, as well as some other items. However, I have worshiped there.

In the new chapel I think you have something of an improvement, but something is yet to be desired. In the few times that I have been present I was able to worship there. Whether that can happen better in the new chapel, I am not quite sure. If so, I am for it. If no, I am not for it. Here are my reasons:

a. We may doll up our places of worship, but still they become more aesthetic experiences than worshipful experiences. I have visited some of the cathedrals of Europe, as you have also. I am frankly skeptical about the worship value there.

b. After all the honest toil you have given in the past years there, I am sure you want to see an efficient seminary plant. I do too. However, I wonder whether or not you are committed to keeping the seminary in Chicago? I

Dan West to Rufus Bowman, August 4, 1945, box 8, Dan West Papers, Brethren Historical Library and Archives.

Authentic Worship | 37

still hope it might move out to the country or some small town. Grant all the arguments in favor of a metropolitan seminary, I think the weight is still in the other direction. If you build a large chapel there, or invest much more money, you are much more likely to stay there.

c. I am thinking about what will happen to the students who come there through the next twenty-five years. With the building up of scholastic standing, I think Bethany may become very respectable someday. If so, I think it will have lost something. I should like to see it down decades the seminary of the little people, and certainly for the little people. If that be valid, we cannot go at these problems in the same way that ambitious religious planners go. And I should dread to see our beloved church become too much like some others that I have seen.

2. What kind of chapel. Suppose all of my item 1 is of lesser value than I think it is, and that you ought to go ahead with your plans. I am concerned about the kind of worship arrangement that is built. Architecturally I think some of the English chapels and other college chapels and university chapels and some others, are suitable for certain types of people, with certain types of religion. I do not think any of them that I have ever seen are suitable for the genius of the Brethren. Some years ago at McPherson I had a good talk with Calvert Ellis. He said then that the Brethren Church has not yet decided whether it is going to build its worship program about a spectacle, or about a fellowship. At the Manchester Conference in June, we talked about it again. He is just as much concerned as I am and highly critical, he said, of the customary patterns toward which we have been moving. So am I, as you knew before.

I should like to see any new developments in worship arrangements wrought out by nontechnical people. I don't know who makes the plans, but I rather guess that architects do chiefly, as they do for school buildings, hospitals, office buildings and others, but I do not think the typical architect will understand the genius of the church as well as some nontechnical people. For that reason I have these suggestions to offer:

a. Let's base our worship on fellowship. I know you agree with that point, but what will it look like architecturally? I think no pulpit, no cross, no stained glass windows, and I am not even sure about the velvet curtain at the front, I am not sure about any raised platform either, and certainly I am not in favor of the aisles leading down to the central point from which some so-called superior person sends out the word of God, or guides in worship. Rather, I much prefer a circle. We have that sort of thing in our summer camps, and I think it is much more fitting than anything that I have seen in chapel arrangement.

b. I think we might borrow from the Quakers something of quiet and plain beauty. Even they have begun to lose faith in their own type of architecture. But I think that is a net loss. In some places they still hold it. Those who object to the so-called "barnlike" structures have an obligation to put up a better arrangement, and I am in favor of the improvement, but the improvement is not in line with keeping up with the Joneses. Maybe we can borrow from some other people, but I hope we do not borrow from the Catholics. The little time I spent in Spain was entirely too long to make me any more appreciative of their way of doing. As a matter of fact, I have some dread that we are following the Catholic pattern already. I could give you instances if you wanted them, but perhaps you don't need them.

c. On money. If the chapel should be built, and if it is the kind of building that fits with the genius of Brethren faith, then I am ready to help in trying to raise the money. Again, I hope we do not get many big contributions from the big people in the church. It is their custom to salve consciences by building churches. Rather, I think we ought to get small contributions from the little people and make it into a real sense, our chapel, our seminary, to serve our church.

Maybe this is really irritating to you, but it is not intended to be any more than the truth. I should be glad to hear from you and to give and take further. Once you convince me of the essential rightness I shall be very happy to cooperate as best I can.

What do you say about another meeting of the Elgin-Bethany staff on the peace question sometime this fall? I shall be very happy to work on it as best I can if you agree.

Cordially yours,
Dan West

PS. Would it be good to make plans for the Brethren to donate some labor as they did in building the cannery down near New Paris? I recognize the problem of union labor and maybe that takes precedence.

Which Emphasis?

In the past fifty years man has learned more about the universe than was known in all previous history. Comparatively we still know less than that about ourselves, but we are learning more. We know very little about God.

Worshiping has more to do with attitudes, human relationships, and purposes. Public prayer (the "soul's sincere desire" sometimes) and other efforts may be of greater importance than our learning and thinking. For effective living, attitudes and knowledge must be made to fit.

How we respond in action to the universe, to people and to God is another emphasis, and the most important one, especially in our changing world. Though different, it must fit our worshiping and our learning. "We live our way into our thinking more than we think our way into our living."

Jesus never asked anybody to understand him or to worship him. But he did ask some to follow him, including us. "Not every one who says to me, 'Lord, Lord,' shall enter the kingdom of heaven, but he who does the will of my Father. . . . Every one then who hears these words of mine and does them will be . . . a wise man" [Matt. 7:21, 24]. "If you love me, you will keep my commandments" [John 14:15].

During World War II Prof. Arthur Holt addressed a group of Mennonites, Friends, and Brethren. He told of the Calvinists, who led Protestant America in the early nineteenth century, emphasizing theology. Later came the Methodist leaders, who emphasized revivals. "Now," he said, "the leadership of America is coming to the historic peace churches. The earlier leaders led with the jaw. These lead with the hands."

If their opportunities had been taken more seriously, his prophecy might have been fulfilled before this time. Yes something has been done, but too little. Maybe they have "come to the kingdom for such a time as this." More minds are opening now than ever before.

No purpose is served in being cynical about anybody's church because of the past. But none has been good enough yet. The future is far more strategic. Unless much more is done now and done much better, we "ain't got long to stay here." The human race can destroy itself quickly.

Dan West, "Which Emphasis?," *Messenger*, April 28, 1966, 32.

Our Brethren forefathers were wise in avoiding creeds. And with all their faults, they were correct in emphasizing doing more than worshiping. And, thank God, they have not yet been nationalized. There is no ground for pride here, just gratitude.

We Christians need one another more than ever before. Every denomination may have something in its culture needed by all the rest; for example, Einstein guessed in 1931 that no war was possible if only two percent refused to fight. But peace requires far more than renouncing war; it also demands sacrifice and patient toil. Bert Roling in *UNESCO Courier* for January 1966 says:

"Many disciplines will have to cooperate to yield some insight: psychology, history, economics, sociology, legal science, and even theology and art history. . . . These play an important part in attitudes and views. . . . These attitudes and views are of greatest importance with respect to war and peace."

If Brethren try hard with Mennonites and Friends to work against war and for peace, others will cooperate. Maybe it is not too late even yet.

Holy Places

The "Holy Land" is a very unholy place now. It has been for centuries, but likely more so since 1948 when it was split between the Arabs and the Israelis. A stone wall runs down through the "Holy City," Jerusalem. It was built there to stop snipers' bullets—or some of them.

At Bethlehem an imposing church has been built over the place where Jesus was supposedly born. And down below in a kind of basement in a small hollow in the wall is placed a kind of gold star to make the exact spot where he was born. But the guide was honest about it—*maybe* this was the place. Some think a cave on the hillside outside of town is more likely the place. But that is not marked, not built up. I wonder what Jesus would say, he walked back there to those two places.

I have wondered what makes any place "holy." It must be the association which we tend to make with some great event; then the event and the place get tied up closely together, and later the place becomes more important than the event itself. This must have happened over the early centuries in the minds of some zealous people who started the Crusades. Then the places where he was born and walked and died and rose were fought over in his name. What would he say about that?

Over in Athens across from the famous Acropolis on another hill slope is a cave with bars and an iron door in front—locked. This is supposed to be the place where Socrates was imprisoned and where he died from drinking the poison which his lawmakers demanded. There is no name, no embellishment—nothing to mark it from any other place where somebody put up bars to keep somebody in—and out. Is that a holy place?

In some of our newer churches the word sanctuary is used. That means a holy place, in the dictionary anyhow. And we may come to believe that this is the place where God is, in spite of the statement by Paul to the Athenians that "God . . . does not live in shrines made by man" (Acts 17:24). I guess he is not boxed up anywhere.

At Hiroshima a very unholy act was committed. The same rule of association would make that a very unholy place. People are still dying apparently

---

Dan West, undated, box 50, Dan West Papers, Brethren Historical Library and Archives.

from the effects of the bomb dropped there nearly fifteen years ago. But the city is remarkably rebuilt now and still not finished. There is a peace memorial there and groups of people are trying to make it a center for peace on earth. Is it possible that the rule can work both ways? Some places can move in meaning from holy to unholy, and another from unholy to holy?

IV.

AMERICAN MATERIALISM

I want a life of social integrity," wrote Dan West in his critique of President Lyndon Johnson's war on poverty. For West, the centrality of Jesus' teaching that a person's worth does not consist in the value of their material possessions was a universal given (see Luke 12:15).

In the second essay, West turned to American experiences during World War II to propose consumer and producer cooperation and intelligent giving as providing purpose for individuals as well as solutions to human problems.

The impact of the social gospel movement on West's life is expressed in the third essay, where he turns to a sermon preached by William Gannett, a well-known Unitarian minister and social reformer.

Let's Start a War on Affluence!

The government has started a war on poverty. That is good. I am all for it. But maybe we ought also to start a war on affluence.

You may prefer only one war at a time. But if poverty and affluence are closely related, neither war can be won separately. With two healthy campaigns at the same time, we might win. Let's start with poverty first.

What is poverty? That looks like an easy one. The government had decided that any family with less than $3,000 a year is in poverty. Recently they upped it somewhat. Using the Agriculture Department's plan with a basic cost of 23 cents per person per meal, a family of four should have at least $3,310 a year. With only three persons in the family, at least $2,440; with two, at least $1,990; for a single person, at least $1,540. Below these figures, people are classed as poor.

But the US Chamber of Commerce holds that dollars are not the best yardstick here, because there are many factors. ". . . [A] small family living in a warm climate and growing most of its own food could live comfortably" on this income. They urged a "market basket" standard—"what it costs to live a decent life in different parts of the country under different circumstances." That does make some sense. But what is a "decent life" and what does it require?

Look at one startling example from outside the USA. Gandhi in his later years had a regular diet of parched corn, goat's milk, and oranges, and he was still going strong until an assassin's bullet stopped him at seventy-eight years. His clothing supply consisted of one shawl and two loincloths plus sandals. The "estate" which he left: three bowls (one of silver), one fork, one spoon, one pair of spectacles, one watch, one letter opener, two pairs of sandals, a New Testament, and a copy of the Bhagavad Gita. Did he have enough for a decent life?

If we see the problem only in American terms, it is somewhat simpler. But from now on we must learn to live in a world. That makes poverty a harder and even more important problem, and there is no quick or easy solution.

Dan West, "Let's Start a War on Affluence!," *Messenger*, January 20, 1966, 20-21.

Poverty can be measured by the difference between what we have and what we want. More than twenty years ago a friend of mine was asked by a businessman whose income had been cut, "How can I live on $47,000 a year?" My friend, whose income may have been less than one-tenth as much, replied, "I don't know."

A college dictionary defines *affluence* as: "Abundance of material goods; wealth." Certainly it means plenty—more than is really needed for a decent life. (People's needs are not all the same.) It may even include some luxuries. "What is wrong about that?" Well, there are dangers. Here are a few warnings:

- from a medieval monk, "Discipline begets abundance. Abundance, unless we use the utmost care, destroys discipline."

- from Prof. J. K. Galbraith, of Harvard University, "Wealth is the relentless enemy of understanding."

- from Prof. A. K. Steigerwalt of the University of Michigan, "In times past and with substantially less material abundance men have had a greater sense of fulfillment and satisfaction than has modern man seated gluttonously in the midst of opulence never before known in the Western world. . . . The corrupting influences stem in great measure from the absence of any philosophic vision of the nature of man and the universe."

- from Jesus, " . . . [The] cares of the world and the delight in riches choke the word" [Matt. 13:22].

Whatever happens in this world, I need some food, some clothing, some shelter—and some other things. With too little I cannot live well. With more I can live more abundantly—up to a certain point. But where is that point?

Take a piece of bread, if you like bread, or strawberry pie if you prefer. When you are hungry, one piece is good—maybe better than that. Maybe the second piece is also good. But the sixth or seventh is not as good as the first or second—even from the same loaf or pie. It might not be good at all, depending on what else has happened before. Economists call this "the law of diminishing returns."

For the most abundant life, I must stop—even though the flavor is good and the hostess or waitress is generous. Other good things—such as clothes, houses, cars—follow the same law. Up to a point more things mean more life. Beyond it they mean less life, even though they always seem to promise more life.

Where is the right place to put a ceiling for anybody who wants to be a whole person in a messed-up world?

People who have more than I have put on heavy pressure toward raising my ceiling. Starving children are less vocal. But I can choose which voices I hear most effectively. If I can hear the cry of starving children right in the middle of reading a menu in a restaurant, I can easily choose powdered milk *for them* instead of strawberry pie a la mode *for me*.

To an increasing number of good-hearted spenders a dollar more or a dollar less does not mean much. But Jane Addams spoke with real insight here, "It is a terrible thing to hold in your hand the power of life or death for another person." A dollar bill has that power.

I want to keep fit now and work hard if possible beyond the age of eighty. And I want a life of personal integrity from now on. Also, I want a life of social integrity from now on. That includes the welfare of all the neighbors whom I want to love as I love myself. Where should be our ceiling for me? It requires giving up some good things for me. If that sacrifice comes out of a hunger and thirst for righteousness and a real love for hungry fellowmen, it produces more abundant life *for us*. Here is where the war on affluence begins—with me.

The enemy we face is not any one person or any group. It is an attitude, affecting many well-intentioned people—rich and poor. These statements tell something about attitudes:

1. "We are getting a new TV set—we have to spend the money somehow" (a lady at home).

2. "As long as I have money, I'll buy clothes. I don't care how much it is" (a teenage girl overheard on a train).

3. "Be thankful that you live in a country with a standard of living that other people envy" (a card in the window of a bank at Thanksgiving time).

4. "The deluxe model costs just the same as the regular one. You just have to pay longer" (a young housewife).

5. "To a very large extent . . . we associate truth with convenience" (J. K. Galbraith).

6. "Christians should be satisfied with less for themselves so that they can share.... I refuse to buy a new dress that I think is pretty because I have plenty of nice clothes now" (a teenage girl in a letter).

7. "Women, give half your wardrobe for peace" (a middle-aged mother).

8. "A man's life does not consist in the abundance of things" [Luke 12:15, adapted] (Jesus).

Attitudes can be changed—never easily—even after youth has passed. Gandhi changed his when he had an income of $20,000 a year—a lot of money in the 1890s. When he was mistreated while trying to help his people in South Africa, he cut loose from his affluent society, identified with the poor, and followed through to his death. If determined Christians change their attitudes in similar ways and about as much, they can do more than he did.

Here is a good prayer to start with:

> Give me neither poverty nor riches;
> feed me with the food that is needful for me,
> lest I be full, and deny thee,
>   and say, "Who is the LORD?"
> or lest I be poor, and steal,
>   and profane the name of my God.
>   —Prov. 30:8*b*-9

While the state is promoting a war on poverty, the church might well prosecute a war on affluence. If the two agencies work together honestly, our emerging world in the imminent future might move noticeably toward the kingdom of God.

Some Economic Disciplines

A discipline is a conscious control toward a purpose. Some controls are always necessary in any kind of a world—more of them in this complex world. During wartime governments always increase the number of external controls for war purposes; Christian living calls for controls which are *self*-imposed or are matters of agreement in voluntary groups.

"Special privilege is never given up; it must be taken away." This axiom of the Marxists is very irritating since it comes so near the truth. We are glad to recognize the brilliant examples of voluntary renunciation of wealth and other special privileges, but I wish they were not so scarce. We need an abundance of group evidence to prove the Marxists wrong here.

Because this economic field has been long neglected by so many well-intentioned people, it needs an extra emphasis now. How we go about it makes much difference, however. In the rainbow-spread of basic assumptions (with family "self-sufficiency" at one end and Hutterite communism at the other), I assume the rightness of family-owned houses and homesteads and with most equipment privately owned. For me the family is basic to all group planning; working on other basic social units must not weaken it, however necessary they are too.

To me the following types of economic disciplines are necessary for responsible living. There may be others such as rent, interest, and insurance—which are not treated here:

1. Self-rationing. "Putting a ceiling on one's own wants." In a world like this, or like the one we want, the sharing of scarce goods and services must be controlled by somebody. If we do not do that ourselves, someone else must do it. If anyone else does it, there is a big chance for the violation of personality in some way. These things can be done, beginning now, which will help:

   a. Measuring family needs in terms of food, clothing, shelter, medical care, etc. (If one does not have family responsibility yet, the job is measuring *personal* needs.) This is hard work, especially when we

---

Dan West, March 4, 1944, and November 18, 1947, box 50, Dan West Papers, Brethren Historical Library and Archives.

include the welfare of other families (persons) in local communities, in geographical regions, in nations, and in "one world." The war compelled the shrinking of "the American standard of living"; the aftermath prevents its restoration—unless we forget the needy world. In the long run we cannot have a very high standard unless we help other peoples to raise their standards first.

b. If a peacetime OPA [Office of Price Administration] returns, accepting it gracefully until a better plan has been developed. This does not always mean enthusiasm for the OPA.

c. Learning from OPA and other efforts at rationing how to develop a better governmental rationing, but especially how to develop the plan of self- and voluntary-group rationing appropriate to Christian living.

Starting from here, our development will likely come in this order: b, c, a. I wish it could be a *and* b *and* c, all at once.

2. Consumer-planning and cooperation. A group job, needed to make cooperation effective and satisfactory, to avoid wasteful advertising and excessive prices resulting from "frozen" or wasted goods, and to build the small community structure out of which a sound world structure can be developed. A known demand is basic to intelligent and efficient producing and distributing, although it is hard on "rugged individuals." "Consumer's choice is the economists' ballot-box."

3. Subsistence farming, etc., where soil is available, not for mere existence, but for abundant living. "Abnormal life begins with the loss of one's own field and dwelling place" ([Albert] Schweitzer). Some people may be unfitted for subsistence farming; if so they should not attempt it. However, most of us would be happier that way. Our commercial world is based on the plan of all workers producing some foods, raw materials, goods or services which will sell best for money with which to buy whatever commodities and services they need for their families. In the next decade, world markets will be especially uncertain and politically controlled; in the world we want, the present commercial pattern will not fit well. Under postwar stresses governments will likely make some undesirable restrictions. Whatever our conditions, our motivation should be that of the soundest plan possible, more than that of fear of want.

4. Producer-planning. Beginning now, I must learn how to avoid being my neighbor's competitor; otherwise, I cannot well object to my country being a neighboring country's competitor. With expanding markets, I can ignore my neighbor across the road and my country can ignore a neighboring country. In a shrinking world market, neither neighbor can be ignored. Locally and nationally, we who produce are either competitors or cooperators—maybe both, but cooperation ought to be the emphasis.

    Disciplines such as group planning for dairy herds to supply a known milk demand, for flocks of sheep or hens, for orchards, etc., are new for most people—to give a few examples. Producer-planning is much harder in the industrial field except under war conditions.

5. Producer-cooperating. Matching tools, implements, and other privately owned goods for the efficient producing of goods for family subsistence and/or for a known market . . . taking responsibility for neighbor's tools and machinery when using them . . . returning them promptly afterwards . . . these and other neighborly practices are good economic disciplines. For example, if the West family needs a team of horses part-time, but should not own them, they have an extra responsibility to the neighbor who owns a team, but who lacks full-time work for them. Again, one good vacuum sweeper in one home matched with one good lawn mower in another home will help to make good neighbors if they are generous and responsible people. A third example: swapping surplus berry plans or seeds—or whatever you have to swap—will also help. Milk producers, fruit producers, war producers have cooperated at least on a limited scale. Creative living requires widening spheres of cooperation in the production of economic goods and services.

6. Distributor-planning. With the high development of transportation and communication, we must choose between competition (and/or wasteful investment) and cooperation—all the way from automobiles in the neighborhood to ships on the sea, and air bases and planes. Whoever controls distribution controls the lives of those who must depend on distribution. "Power-state" governments will likely control most transportation in the next decades.

7. Responsible buying. When I make a purchase, all of these questions need answers:

   a. Do I need this article for effective living?
   b. Is it better to buy it than to make it or grow it?
   c. Is the quality good (at least)?
   d. Is the price fair to me—not too high?
   e. Is the price high enough to be fair to everyone who has put genuine value into it?
   f. If the price is too high everywhere, is this the lowest price—without spending too much time and energy looking elsewhere?
   g. On goods that last a while, will I like them after the novelty has worn off?
   h. Can I easily keep fellowship with the poor after I have it?
   i. A purchase is a vote for the continuance of a certain firm and business. Do I believe this firm and business ought to continue?

   Unless I can answer "yes" to questions a, b, f, and g, I will not buy. I feel better when I can answer "yes" to c, d, e, and h. I feel best when I can answer "yes" to all of them. Number e is hard, but I must try to answer it.

8. Responsible selling of goods or services. When I make a sale, all of these questions need answers:

   a. Can I spare this article, house, farm, service, etc.?
   b. Is the quality known to the buyer?
   c. Is the price (wage) fair to me—not too low?
   d. Is the price (wage) fair to the purchaser (employer)—not too high?
   e. If the prevailing price is too high, can I share with him in wholesome, neighborly ways?
   f. If it is too low, can I get him to share some of the profits with me?
   g. Am I avoiding competition with another near neighbor who has similar goods or services to sell? Someday I must reduce competition with far neighbors too.
   h. Will my obligations to producers' cooperatives, labor unions, or other organizations fit with "brotherhood economics" here?
   i. Could this type of sale be made to close friends and around the world without leading to war or to unwholesome living?

Unless I can answer "yes" to questions a and b, I will not sell (except number a under necessity). If I can answer "yes" to questions c, d, e, g, and h, I will feel better. I feel best when I can answer "yes" to all of them.

9. Responsible saving. For future growth and for the rainy day. These questions are important:

   a. Does my family's need make a claim on this surplus of goods or money?
   b. In the light of the *present* world's needs for food, clothing, shelter, medical care, recreation, etc., do I have a right to save for my family's *future* needs?
   c. Is this the best way to save (e.g., maybe I can save better by furnishing capital for someone else to start up with)?
   d. Can I be reasonably sure to avoid exploitation of other people by this form of saving (e.g., the investment of my life insurance premiums)?
   e. Are my plans for saving reasonably close to my probable future needs?

   Unless I can answer "yes" to a, b, and e I won't plan to save. If I can answer "yes" to all of them I feel at ease on this point.

10. Intelligent giving.

    a. Is this need genuine?
    b. Is *giving* the best way to meet this need, as contrasted with *giving opportunity* for self-help?
    c. Can I rightly spare the goods, services, or money to meet this need?
    d. Can I give without damaging the self-respect of the receiver?
    e. Can I give without feeling "bighearted"? Playing Santa Claus really is risky for the actor.
    f. Will this gift in this way help the receiver to carry his own burden?
    g. Is the middleman between me and the receiver (if there must be one) efficient in management and socially responsible in policy?
    h. Should I give *now*?

    Unless I can say "yes" to a and b I won't give. I had better be able to say "yes" to all of them.

These economic disciplines for both persons and smaller groups are steps to national disciplines.

"Down in their hearts, wise men know this truth: The only way to help yourself is to help others"—Elbert Hubbard, a philosopher who went down on the [Lusitania].

Drudgery

Play gives us what we want directly. Work holds a promise ahead of us, but drudgery neither gives what we want nor offers real promise. It's something that just has to be done and it is unpleasant.

More than half a century ago William Gannett preached a sermon "Blessed Be Drudgery" and he insisted that culture comes through this drudgery. Then he listens to somebody's growl: "Culture through my drudgery! . . . Keeping house or keeping accounts, tending babies, teaching primary school, weighing sugar and salt at a counter, those blue overalls in the machine shop (or on the farm, D. W.)—have these anything to do with 'culture'? Culture takes leisure, elegance, wide margins of time, a pocketbook; drudgery means limitations, coarseness, crowded hours, chronic worry, old clothes, black hands, headaches. Culture implies college: life allows a daily paper, a monthly magazine, the circulating library, and two gift-books at Christmas. Our real and our ideal are not twins—never were! I want the books, but the clothes basket wants me. The two children are good, and so would be two hours a day without the children. I crave an outdoor life, and walk downtown of mornings to perch on a high stool till suppertime. I love nature, and figures are my fate. My taste is books, and I farm it. My taste is art, and correct exercises. My taste is science, and I measure tape. I am young and like stir: the business jogs on like a stagecoach. Or I am *not* young, I am getting gray over the ears, and like to sit down and be still; but the drive of the business keeps both tired arms stretched out full length. . . . I did not choose my calling, but was dropped into it—by my innocent conceit—or by duty to the family—or by a parent's foolish pride—or by our hasty marriage; or a mere accident wedged me into it. Would I could have my life over again! Then, whatever I *should* be, at least I would *not* be what I am today!"

After listening [Gannett] insists, "Our *prime* elements are due to our drudgery . . . . When we were small, Mother had a way of harping on them, and Father joined in emphatically, and the minister used to refer to them in church. . . . [These] *are* the very qualities which the mothers tried to tuck into us when they tucked us into bed . . . . Father and mother and the ancestors

Dan West, August 1, 1944, box 47, Dan West Papers, Brethren Historical Library and Archives.

before them have done much to bequeath those elemental qualities to us; but that which scrubs them into us, the clinch which makes them actually ours, and keeps them ours, and adds to them as the years go by—that depends on our own plod, our plod in the rut, our drill of habit; in one word, depends upon our 'drudgery.' It is because we have to go, and *go*, morning after morning, through rain, through shine, through toothache, headache, heartache to the appointed spot, and do the appointed work; because, and only because, we have to stick to that work through the eight or ten hours, long after rest would be so sweet; because the schoolboy's lesson must be learnt at nine o'clock without a slip; because the accounts on the ledger must square to a cent; because the goods must tally exactly with the invoice; because good temper must be kept with children, customers, neighbors, not seven, but seventy times seven times; because the besetting sin must be watched today, tomorrow, and the next day; in short, without much matter *what* our work be, whether this or that, it is because, and only because, of the rut, plod, grind, humdrum *in* the work, that we at last get those self-foundations laid of which I spoke—attention, promptness, accuracy, firmness, patience, self-denial, and the rest."

It is hard for people of leisure to believe in the necessity of drudgery but most of the people of the earth know it well because they have little time for leisure. The requirements of getting food and clothing and shelter take too nearly all of their time. And it has always been so. Had we been able to avoid the war we might have had with science and invention the blessings of the shiny new mechanical tools to do most of our drudgery. Maybe someday the common people can have them. But the problem of food for the next two decades will not depend so much on tractors as it will on drudgery with simpler tools—unless we want and are willing to fit in with the political system which controls the power tools.

This shows up in CPS [Civilian Public Service] camps sharply. Intelligent men with consciences against killing reason logically: With a bulldozer to handle dirt by the yard, why bother with a shovel? But if the bulldozer is "needed" for war purposes, the CPS men have to use the shovel. If the air drill is "needed," they will have to use the tempered bar and sledge. This sometimes causes acute suffering and frustration. One of the hardest lessons for an intellectual to learn is the necessity of much drudgery in a world like this.

The next hard lesson is to get and hold some deep meaning to all this drudgery. The Nazis learned how to do it and so did the Communists; then people willingly and cheerfully underwent all kinds of hardship for the sake of their cause.

Christians have been much slower to learn this. During the cathedral building age part of it got done but not in recent centuries. This is the task of the church; to develop a better cause than the Communists have produced; to be honest with all the persons who have to do the drudgery and then to show those who must endure it the essential meaning. This means getting closer to the poor, and sharing their burdens. It means spreading the necessary drudgery and eliminating the unnecessary drudgery. It means recognizing the respectable Christian who condemns his brethren to drudgery he will not help to bear as a sinner—however good may be his intentions. If the church can do this it can bring labor to the rightful place—not as a curse but as a necessity for abundant life now, in both physical and spiritual terms. Once we have shared drudgery *willingly* we may build a world where life can be abundant on a higher plane.

V.

HEIFER PROJECT

D**an West is primarily known** as the founder of the humanitarian agency Heifer International. Inspired by experiences as an aid worker with the American Friends Service Committee during the Spanish Civil War, Dan West founded Heifer Project—now Heifer International—as a Church of the Brethren relief program during World War II. A precursor to World War II, the Spanish Civil War was a conflict of considerable brutality with atrocities committed by both the fascist-backed forces of Francisco Franco and the communist-backed Republican forces. As the conflict unfolded, West became convinced that immediate handouts of aid were inadequate to meet long-term human needs. What people needed were actual sources of human nourishment such as dairy cattle. This vision is mirrored in a 1938 letter to his wife, Lucy, while West served in Spain, as well as his report to the larger church in *Gospel Messenger* published later that year.

In the third document, from 1945, West asserts that Heifer Project was rooted in the life and teachings of Jesus and hence fundamentally religious in character.

The final document is a list of objectives West wrote for Heifer Project in 1958 and 1961. West insists that while working with other humanitarian agencies, Heifer should maintain its nonprofessional people-to-people approach and be willing to pass out of existence when its mission has been completed.

Letter to Lucy West

On the Train
Barcelona—Valencia
January 11, 1938

My Lucy,

This is the end of a meaningful day. The bright sunshine, almost like May back home, is most welcome. The stars last night, and tonight, shine intensely against the dark sky, even with the moonlight. The city is big—1,100,000, modern and beautiful—wide smooth streets and fine houses, except in the slums; and if there were no war one might spend a delightful time here, amid palms and oranges, big roses, and such.

But I have had a heavy meal of suffering—enough for one day. In the seminary where formerly Catholic priests were trained, live 2,500 refugees, in a moderate-sized room. One hundred in a long large room, some trying to keep up family life but many going to pieces in every way. For three or four months this has been used for refugees, and considering everything, it is fairly clean—my nose wasn't seriously offended.

The building with several stories and three inner courts is very beautiful. The money and labor, and perhaps hope, put into visible form might be justified if the priests who came through their training had really been helpful to the problems of people. It is four centuries since Loyola, and more than ten since Christianity had a strong foothold here. That is long enough. A church with a chance like that can be indicted for not doing its duty. And I can understand the fury of those who want to be rid of it.

The only place incense arises now is in the kitchen; and that is the steam from the hot soup. The soup looks good—chickpeas and rice, but it would not make a satisfactory meal. 220 pounds of chickpeas and 165 pounds of rice go into soup for 2,500 people—that is 2½ ounces of the mixed foods per person—and each one gets about 30 grams (two ordinary slices) of dark bread;

Dan West to Lucy West, January 11, 1938, box 2, Dan West Papers, Brethren Historical Library and Archives.

that is all for their noon meal; and only the 280 children there get anything in the morning. For supper they have beans and another chunk of bread. And I guess there is little else that anyone gets. One mother was sitting on a bed with twelve to fifteen oranges around her—they must have a bit of money.* I suppose the menu varies a bit, but not much.

As we were leaving the upstairs open corridor—lovely stone pillars and rounded arches—I noticed a pile of bones lying near the wall. It looked as though someone had had several chickens. I asked our guide (an official) about it. "No," he said. They were the bones of cats—and they were picked clean. When any of the folks can catch a cat, they have a bit more to eat.

The whole thing nearly took my appetite for lunch. At the end of a simple meal, not too much but several times what these poor people had at the Seminary Refuge, I couldn't eat my orange. I wanted to find two hungry children, divide it, give each one half, and hold them in my arms for another picture. But we couldn't well arrange it. And so I asked Norma Jacob to give it to a mother of seven children—one is three months old—who came to the house for some food tonight. She gave it to one of the children (two to three years old) who came along. I feel much better than if I had eaten it.

Dearie, I am grateful that we are able to feed our children all they need. It makes me humble, too.

If you still make copies of my letters to send out over there, will you send one to Jim Erbaugh. Maybe he will want to give to help the children.

Please send to Alfred Jacob (address on letterhead) several booklets on child feeding and care soon. If necessary, please pay and ask USA Dept. of Agriculture to send direct.

Your Dan

*No water for washing clothes in the seminary. I don't know where that is done. No soap, of course, and yet I was surprised to see some of the clothes fairly clean.

Saving Lives in Spain and China

Civil war has been destroying the country that was Spain. Two years ago twenty-four million persons lived there, but more than a million have been killed. More than a million soldiers—perhaps 600,000 on each side—are now attempting to destroy each other. There are said to be three million refugees, and more than a million of them are children.

This bitter struggle grew out of a deep-seated conflict between classes; it is part of an old story, too. This is the third civil war in slightly over a century. Whatever the merits of either party, now it is an endurance test with suffering increasing on both sides. Several times there has been talk of some kind of an armistice, but it has not happened yet. Meanwhile the killing goes on and hunger takes a growing toll of the lives of innocents.

How We Got Started

Early in 1936 several English Quakers were concerned about beginning good-will work in Madrid, but after the war broke out that could not happen. And so efforts were made to help care for the children in and around Barcelona. Several influential Spaniards also became interested in the possibility of help and in a short time there grew the English Quaker Service. From England in October 1936, came word for help from America. After some thinking and planning together by representatives of the Friends, Brethren, Mennonites, and the Federal Council of Churches, Sylvester Jones was sent to see about the need and the chances for nonpartisan work on both sides of the conflict. When his report was approved one worker was sent to each side in May of 1937. Others have been sent since as the work has developed.

The Workers

At present there are twelve workers from America in Spain in the cooperative project, nine on the Loyalist (government) side and three on the Insurgent (Franco) side. Three of them are Dunkers. Miss Martha Rupel works at the hospital in Murcia (Loyalist Spain). She has been there since early August. David Blickenstaff has his headquarters at Bilbao; he has been there since

---

Dan West, "Saving Lives in Spain and China," *Gospel Messenger*, December 17, 1938, 12, 15.

early December 1937. Paul Bowman sailed from New York on October 28, to work with him on the Franco side.

Over here is a Committee on Spain with headquarters at 20 South 12th Street, Philadelphia, Pennsylvania. It is composed of several Friends, Mrs. R. D. Murphy, M. R. Zigler, and Dan West from our church, Orie Miller of the Mennonite Central Committee, and Roswell Barnes of the Federal Council. John Reich, the secretary, carries the main burden of the work. The Friends Service Council of London has workers in Barcelona, Murcia, and elsewhere. We consider ourselves a unit with them as our peace testimony is one, and so are our essential purposes. The Spaniards call us all "Quaqueros," and they are grateful for the help we are giving their children.

The Work

Many outside agencies are helping there, and both governments have extensive plans to save the suffering civilians. But it is wartime and all that every agency can do will not keep them all alive. How many must die this winter no one knows—but thousands certainly, likely tens of thousands. Since they cannot all be saved we have developed the policy: "Save the children first"—the neediest children in the neediest places in the neediest regions. This means refugee children on each side first, who are far from home and most helpless. Dependent mothers and old people are cared for, too, but not first. On the Loyalist side the need is far greater; and so we are doing more there. Because of the different conditions, we are maintaining some hospitals, colonies, workshops, and schools, but they are not first; and we are not expanding these. We must save the children first, and that means feeding them first. As winter comes on we will give out clothing—to the neediest children first.

On the Franco side we worked most in the mountains of the north last winter. (It was colder weather than Chicago had.) In the spring we worked along the Ebro near Belchite, Lleida, and Teruel—the neediest places. On the Loyalist side we are working in and around Barcelona and Murcia. The former territory is filled with refugees from northern Spain who come over through France more than a year ago. The English workers are still doing most of it there. Our work is done mostly in the region around Murcia where refugees have come there from central and southern Spain. Perhaps that is the neediest region of the whole country as most of the other agencies from outside Spain are not working there.

A Bit of the Need

In a letter from Murcia, September 27, Florence Conard writes: "Some time ago I was at the hospital for supper with the English nurses. After the meal, they slipped into the babies' room to see a little tyke that they didn't think would last the night. The child was supposed to be suffering from kidney trouble, but was actually an excellent example of a typical 'war baby.' It was about six months old, its head one third of all its tiny body. Its arms, I'm not exaggerating, were no bigger around than my forefinger and its loosely covered fingers just hung from the wrists. Its eyes and cheeks were sunken and its jaw and cheekbones were so prominent as to seem completely naked of skin. Already it had begun to gasp a bit for breath, moving its head back and forth on the pillow as though the very motion would give it more air. Calcium was lacking in its body among other things. No bomb holes, or refugees, or women's tears and sob stories can move me so much as that struggling little life, so helpless against external diabolical forces. Just a PS, the baby died."

Never before have I known what food really meant. Not roast pork and mashed potatoes, not good American ice cream, not even spinach and lettuce and cabbage—just food, with no particular taste or form—fuel and nourishment for the weakening flesh.

Bread! Only now am I beginning to understand the meaning of "Give us this day our daily bread" [Matt. 6:11]. Perhaps our "daily bread" today is not 100 grams—3½ ounces, but father and mother will pool their grams, forget their hunger, and give the extra pieces to the young ones. Tomorrow, God willing, "our daily bread" may be 150 grams. We cannot bear to think that perhaps tomorrow there will be no bread. It may be wiser not to think of the morrow. "Give us this day our daily bread."

Not long ago ten, long-looked-for tons of wheat arrived. The men staggered in under the weight of the big sacks and dumped them in limp piles in our warehouse. The little puffs of dust that squirted out from between the sacks as they fell, seemed to hang still and golden on the air. Yesterday the bread from the wheat came in—good bread, brown bread, wheat bread, symbol of health and strength and work, of plenty and friendship and peace.

Heifers for Relief

Little children everywhere need milk or its equivalent. If they get enough of it, they live. If not, tuberculosis or some other disease sweeps them off quickly. The "Heifer Project" is based on this need.

The idea came out of a conversation in Murcia, Spain, in January 1938. In a milk dispensary, D. Parke Lantz, a Mennonite missionary working there as a relief worker, was explaining the plan of feeding babies of the vicinity. Powdered milk from Holland was mixed with water, drawn off in small bottles (no caps on them), and sent home with a waiting relative to feed every one of the 197 babies which the dispensary doctor had put on the approved list. If no one came for the milk for a given child, his name was taken off in favor of a child not yet on the list. Later in some places a baby which did not gain in weight was taken off the list to die.

The milk supply was too small and too uncertain and the food value of the gift from overseas always ended there. Why not bring cows over also so that more children are few and the people are able to help themselves? The grass grows there too when it rains.

A few weeks later the editor of one of the British Labor Party papers in London spoke favorably: "I know where you can get some cows and we will help. By the way, you are not going to give any of those cows to the Franco side, are you?"

"Sure, the children are hungry over there, too."

"Well, if you give one cow to Franco, we won't help to get any of them."

"Sorry—looks as though we can't work together on this."

Franco's representative over here was interested but chiefly in beef cattle. No one else took up the idea.

In the *American Friend* for May 13, 1941, was an article by Kenneth Boulding on "The Economics of Reconstruction." He thought that after the war the dairy population in Europe might be down to 40 percent or even 20 percent of prewar figures. At their rate of cattle production that would mean four—possibly eight or more years until enough milk would be available there. But starving children cannot wait so long—.

Dan West, September 20, 1945, Dan West Biographical File, Brethren Historical Library and Archives.

By November 1941 the Belgians were suffering heavily; their ambassador was eagerly interested in any possibility of milk for them. Of course, we would have to wait until after the war and after the emergency foods and medical supplies were sent over. But the Belgian farmer builds his whole economy around his cow. "If you can get ships—."

Officials in the US Department of Agriculture thought it a practicable idea. There was no doubt about the need in Europe and no doubt either about the source of most of the cows—America. Ship in? One official said, "Maybe your group will decide whether the government will furnish the ships or not." Another wanted to know if they were a git [foolish person]. "All right if you are not going to sell them." One expert urged, "Don't send overseas any cows giving milk. The trip will be too hard on them. Better ship heifers a few months before they come fresh; you get two animals there that way." Thus, heifers instead of cows.

In June 1942 the Brethren Service Committee (Dunkers) approved the plan in principle and founded the Heifer Project Committee. They hoped that milk products at least might come out of the plan.

"Faith"

In the spring of 1943 a new Guernsey calf in the herd of Virgil Mock of New Paris, Indiana, offered him a chance to do something. After a little consultation he sent her in a trailer to O. W. Stine of Millersburg to be raised for relief. Claire, fifteen years old, liked calves and agreed to do the work; his dad to pay the feed bill.

Faith was ear-tagged on May 7, 1943. The aluminum tag carried the number "1," and on the other "Brethren Service Committee."

Other people became interested; hundreds of heifers were tagged and the movement grew. But the war still went on with no promise from anyone that any heifers would be shipped. Most of the donors thought of Belgium as the destination of their gifts.

Out of another beginning ("C.O.'s in the Caribbean," *Christian Century*, August 29, 1945) came a plan to send Faith and fifteen others to the chronic poor in Puerto Rico. The donors were consulted and found willing. On July 12, 1944, they were sent from Mobile to San Juan. Faith was given to a large family living in a poor little house near the sea. The Farm Security Administration had placed her and took the responsibility for her welfare. She gave milk in abundance and ten children had all they could drink. Later when one of our men visited the place, her little calf, a heifer, was not to be seen. Inquiring, he learned that the family thought so much of her that they kept her in the house and carried her out to the cow when she was hungry. That heifer will likely be giving milk by next summer and Faith still goes on helping the children to grow stronger and bigger.

A second shipment of fifty heifers and five bulls went to Puerto Rico in May 1945. Of the total only one animal has died since arriving on the island. The rest are likely well acclimated by this time.

The Records So Far

For years we worked with Belgian officials, but the overturn of the [Hubert] Pierlot regime stopped that. A year ago we were planning to ship 150 heifers to Spain, but some officials in Spain suspected an economic beach head. It failed.

Out of pressure from donors whose heifers had freshened and from other beginnings we sent two small shipments (thirty-four heifers) to Arkansas, one to Pine Bluff in cooperation with the Farm Foundation, another to Cotton Plant in cooperation with the Southern Tenant Farmers Union. Recently one official from the STFU wrote, "I am glad that the Church of the Brethren is helping to Christianize, civilize, and educate my people in Africa and Asia, but I want to ask you to also consider those here at your door. If the Church of the Brethren will help the poor, downtrodden exploited people of my race in the Deep South to get the "Four Freedoms," that work will stand here as a monument to you Christians until stars have been marshaled for burial and funeral torches of burning worlds; and that work will cause the colored people in Africa and Asia to have more faith in the white missionaries sent to them from America."

We also sent four Jersey heifers and one bull to a village in Mexico last spring. The first "heifers" to cross the ocean were bulls. The Near East Foundation wants to improve the native cattle of Greece by sending superior pure-bred bulls from America. After failing to find what they wanted they appealed to the Heifer Project Committee. Ben G. Bushong of Columbia, Pennsylvania, found six fine Brown Swiss bulls, bought them for us, rode in the cattle cars to Saint John, New Brunswick, and put them on the ship after they were consecrated by a Greek Orthodox priest!

Soldiers and travelers in France have brought conflicting reports. "They are well fed." "They are not." Both are correct—in different parts. The "little people" of Alsace are in dire need. Our first European shipment of heifers (130 Holsteins and twenty Guernseys) sailed from Baltimore for Le Havre on September 6, 1945. B. G. Bushong at this end and Eldon Burke in France did most of the work after the heifers reached the Roger Roop farm near Union Bridge, Maryland.

We have made arrangements with UNRRA [United Nations Relief and Rehabilitation Administration] and Polish officials to ship 150 Holstein heifers to Poland soon, to be distributed by Spolem, the national Polish cooperative. More than 180 heifers are waiting at the Roop farm to be shipped if qualified.

Seagoing Cowboys

On May 31, 1945, UNRRA announces their purpose to ship to needy countries in that organization 25,000 heifers and 25,000 horses in the following eighteen months to meet *one percent* of the estimated needs. Good news to us. After the long wait our heifers had a chance to go. Six hundred Brown Swiss heifers were purchased to be sent to the Near East. Lacking cattlemen to care for this livestock on their ships, UNRRA asked the Heifer Project Committee to take that responsibility. We agreed to man the boats during the remainder of 1945. The first ship sailed from Baltimore on June 26.

Up to September 15 more than two hundred men had left American shores in livestock ships carrying more than five thousand animals. The plan is to continue through the winter with ten ships going out every month. If the arrangement is satisfactory to both parties the Heifer Project Committee will try to find qualified men to care for the animals on the sea. We have no responsibility for the distribution of any animals but our own.

In the Future

We are working on plans to ship some of our heifers to Italy this autumn, possibly to Belgium and China and the Ukraine and to Germany and Holland—anywhere the little children need milk and where the cows can be well placed and cared for. There are risks, delays, disease, and accident—but after taking all precautions we go ahead in the hope of saving human life.

How We Work

Many persons have asked how we work. Briefly, thus:

1. A person or group who want to give a heifer selects a good one at any age, usually two to six months—either grade or purebred—Holstein, Guernsey, or Jersey usually—and notifies the project committee or a representative.

2. At a convenient time she is ear-tagged with a serial number and records are made and sent in. She gets good care but is not pampered.

3. One lone heifer in a community cannot be sent abroad—too costly. We urge finding a small group (ten or more) within a community, they are tagged in California, Washington, New York, Virginia, and places between.

4. A local committee, usually from the same church, takes full responsibility for all heifers until they are called for and put on a truck or car for shipment at 18-25 months of age.

5. Tests for tuberculosis and Bang's disease are made by local veterinarians and papers are sent along with the cattle.

6. They are assembled at Roop's farm at our expense.

7. Any gifts of heifers not sent may be exchanged locally or sold for cash to purchase other suitable heifers.

8. UNRRA or the receiving governments pay the costs, to the destination.

9. They are distributed by churches, by cooperatives, by governments, by special committees, or by ourselves to the neediest who are able to care for them.

Who Helps?

The Church of the Brethren is so small and the need so great that we have never thought of going far with the project all by ourselves. Already the Fellowship of Reconciliation, the Rural Life Association, the Evangelical Reformed Church, the Catholic Rural Life Conference are helping officially. Some other churches are helping unofficially and others are interested. One enthusiast spoke thus: "Why, the country people could do the labor and the city people could pay the costs. When the heifers are ready to go, everybody could go to the church in the country, heifers too. They would all worship together and then the heifers would be sent to do good . . . . The Christians of American can save Europe." They can.

In His Name

The movement is basically a religious one in purpose. It is one expression of a deep desire to save the bodies, minds, and souls of the needy children and mothers anywhere in this groping world, a service to "the least of these"—in the Master's name.

Anyone desiring it, can secure more information from the Heifer Project Committee, Nappanee, Indiana.

HPI Objectives for the Next Ten Years

1. Raise and hold the highest standards of quality of animals, wherever possible.

2. Plant more heifers, bulls, pigs, goats, chicks, etc., in the neediest places on earth.

3. Accept no political, religious, or other unnecessary barriers. Needs and resources are our chief determiners.

4. Reach as far toward the neediest families as we can, remembering that the very neediest are not able to care well for the animals.

5. Depend on local committees to select recipients, except where local agencies, such as orphanages, indicate appropriateness. One item: Their goals and methods converge with ours.

6. Send qualified persons with all major shipments, except where our central values can be served otherwise, to help interpret meanings: e.g., heifers to Moscow, 1956.

7. Maintain our people-to-people pattern and nonprofessional tone throughout our work.

8. Urge all recipients to pass on the gift indefinitely by sharing the first heifer calf or other animal with another needy family. Exceptions only where impossible.

9. Encourage literate recipients to write to donors—and donors to reply.

10. Develop hearty team spirit and the techniques with agencies such as CWS [Church World Service], Ag. Missions, FAO [Food and Agricultural Organization of the United Nations], Peace Corps wherever their policies converge with ours.

11. Maintain tension on all member agencies appropriate to their ability to help.

Dan West, March 1958 and November 1961, Dan West Biographical File, Brethren Historical Library and Archives.

12. Maintain tension on transportation and distributing agencies toward the most efficient service possible. Target: *gifts* of service too, just as animals and cash are given.

13. Encourage establishment of indigenous HPI [Heifer Project International] organizations in Europe, Asia, Africa, and Latin America as fast as local persons and agencies can carry the burden.

14. Continue working in any major country (where we do major work) up to the point where indigenous agencies can carry on the work: e.g., no more chicks needed in South Korea.

15. Pass out of the picture when HPI is no longer needed.

16. Cooperate with research agencies where possible and create our own research pattern where necessary.

In more concrete terms—

1. Better cattle on a million more grassy hills.

2. Better goats and sheep on a million more weedy hills.

3. Better hogs in a million more fertile valleys.

4. Better chickens in ten million more flocks.

5. Better ducks on ten million more ponds—and for good measure.

6. Better bees flying all over the place, to pollinate blossoms and produce honey.

VI.

PEACE IN OUR WORLD
AND IN OUR HOMES

For Dan West, the central human problem was not hunger but war. Inspired in part by William James' essay "The Moral Equivalent of War," West rejected the notion that war was inevitable. As an optimistic progressive rooted in the social gospel, he believed change was both desirable and possible. For him, the rejection of war began at home in the Church of the Brethren and among their allies in the historic peace churches. War, in effect, was a human problem capable of human solutions. Still West's ethic was decidedly centered on Christ. It was about "building the kingdom of God according to the mind of Christ," as he states in a 1939 essay from *The Gospel Messenger*.

Ending war began in the homes of ordinary people and within faith communities, not with governmental elites. West believed the Christian home, particularly the Brethren home, was the primary agent in ending warfare. As usual, West emphasized the immediate and the practical. Heifer Project gave flesh to this vision by empowering families and local communities to become agents of meaningful social change.

In West's writings on peace education, the violent portions of the Hebrew Scriptures and other apocalyptic writings were to be de-emphasized, especially among young children, and heroes of peace and conflict resolution were to be celebrated. And God was to be honored as a loving patriarch. As with other writers of the time, the middle-class nuclear family and conventional gender relationships were assumed norms. West had a decidedly mid-twentieth century vision, but his core conviction that peacebuilding begins with one-on-one human relationships and then proceeds to the local community and beyond is still relevant today.

Am I a Conscientious Objector?

You are probably not a CO—

1. If you believe, down deep in your heart, that there may well be some situations in which it would be God's will for you to take part in war.

2. If you believe that Americans should be prepared to fight, if necessary, for the things we hold dear. If you would be willing to have a bomb dropped on Moscow or some other city in order to "save" your hometown.

3. If you would be willing to join the army in case the American shores were invaded or if a civil war should break out again in this country.

4. If you are willing to work in a job that helps the war effort directly—such as making guns or bombs.

5. If, while earnestly seeking God's will for your life, you believe it is his will for you not to be a CO.

You probably are a CO—

1. If you believe, down deep in your heart, that "all war is sin," and that God's will, as revealed in Jesus, demands a better way to settle disputes.

2. If you believe that America should spend her resources for finding and going this "better way"—to the point where there is nothing left over for military preparations.

3. If you believe that a truly Christian America would refuse to drop any bomb on Moscow or on any other city—even "in self-defense."

4. If you would refuse to work in any job that contributes *directly* to a war effort (such as making guns or bombs), even if such refusing would mean real sacrifice for you.

5. If you are earnestly seeing God's will for your life and believe that it is his will for you to be a CO.

Dan West, "Am I a Conscientious Objector?," *Gospel Messenger*, October 1, 1955, 21.

To be a CO you do not need—

1. To be actually perfect—although we are commanded in that direction. See Matt. 5:48.

2. To know exactly what you would do if your family were attacked by a maniac—although you should have some kind of answer if you are asked this question.

3. To know what the Russian government would do if the American government would quickly become pacifist. Nobody knows the correct answer to this question, as there has never been a large-scale, longtime effort to try pacifism.

4. To renounce the whole idea of police force. One may observe that police always are supposed to be subject to law and to handle the individual criminal, instead of destroying other people and their property—also that policemen do not fight one another as armies do.

Brethren Convictions in Time of War

When things go smoothly our convictions are not so likely to be clear as in times of crisis. Now in the present increasing strain in the whole world we need to know what we believe and how deeply we believe those things. It may be good to consider first what Brethren convictions are not:

1. It is *not* in keeping with any Christian conviction for us to believe that we ought to *save our own sons first.* There is a real instinct for self-preservation, but nobody can find any such emphasis in the New Testament.

2. It is *not* in keeping with Brethren convictions to join the movement to stop Hitler, or [Neville] Chamberlain, or anyone else by military and other coercive measures. It is genuinely pathetic to see how good people in England, Canada, and the United States have fallen in with the temper of the times, have become emotional about the supposedly recent and one-man cause of the European war, and have subtly or openly become eager to stop Hitler by killing German youth and others. Even when our deep desires are thwarted, we must respect personality. We must *love* our enemies.

3. It is *not* in keeping with Brethren convictions to *put our government first.* This is one of the most difficult points to make clear, because we love our country and because we believe in our government. We care deeply for the welfare of our government, especially in times of crisis. But nobody who searches for the meaning of Christ can find any justification for putting any government first. It was not so in the Roman Empire, during the first and second centuries; it was not so in Germany of seventeen hundred and after; it is not so in Germany, Britain, Canada, America, Scandinavia, or in Nigeria, Shansi, or Bombay Provinces. So long as there is no essential conflict, we can follow Christ *and* our government. But when the ways part we must put our Master first and follow him.

As I see it, Brethren convictions do include these *in the following order*:

1. We must give our *clearest testimony to our Christian faith* in our time and place at any price. If we make this conviction central, it orients us for an attitude and a program different from customary attitudes and programs—inside churches and outside, too. If we are ever driven back from imple-

---

Dan West, "Brethren Convictions in Time of War," *Gospel Messenger*, November 4, 1939, 12-13.

menting other precious values, here is our last stand. It was so in the first and second centuries, in the eighteenth, and it must be so in our own century.

2. *Building the kingdom of God* according to the mind of Christ. Our convictions up to the present have had a negative emphasis. Perhaps that was necessary because our spiritual forefathers did not have the opportunity to see as we can see. Also they lived in a less complex world than we live in. We have no reason for censuring them, but in our time and place it is highly unlikely that we can give our clearest possible testimony to our Christian faith unless we become positive and so fulfill the implications of that doctrine.

Our freedom of citizenship in America gives us an extra chance and extra responsibility to further implement our faith. Right now we can help to keep our country from going to war. Neither the old nor the new propaganda nor anything else should be allowed to make us see the war in Europe as one of the angels versus the devils. If we stay out of it we can help to establish a just peace, and save democracy at home and abroad. Then we shall have a greater chance to rebuild the world.

If we do not like the kind of world in process of building by the Nazis, the Communists, or the rugged individualists, we are under increasing obligation to build a world according to the teaching of Jesus. This must be one of our basic convictions for the future. And we must work as long as we have freedom to work.

3. After the two convictions just given, we have an obligation to *save our youth and our church from any unnecessary suffering*. If we are stupid, or obstinate, or scared, we are likely to do unwise things, which may bring suffering to our youth and to our church organizations—for other reasons than our convictions. If we are well-grounded in these convictions, if we are kind, reasonable, and unafraid, it is more likely that we can expect the continuance of our organization and a minimum of suffering for the young men who may have to face the question of military service. We are making wrong assumptions if we think that everyone who opposes us is necessarily devilish, even though we may have to be sure that he is wrong. Healthy minds do not seek martyrdom.

4. After conserving these values, if all three are possible, it is one of our convictions that we must *save our governments* (national, state, and local) *and our neighbors from any unnecessary embarrassment*. To put this value first would destroy any noticeable Christian flavor, but to leave it out would be

genuine ingratitude and would indicate a breaking from the society in which we live and move and have our being.

If we want to be in union of spirit with those who differ profoundly from us, and if we want to accept any responsibility for building an organized society on a Christian basis, we need to plan and work cooperatively with our governments at every point possible for Christian consciences. Also we must give them the benefit of the doubt wherever it does not violate our consciences; and then compensate noticeably where our consciences compel us to part from any government or community policy. If the spirit of community has to be broken, it must not be we who break it.

All along I have been trying to think in terms not only of Brethren in America but in every country in the modern world in case any of us should happen to be found there. Also I am remembering that Brethren have no corner on these convictions. Because our religion is not a religion of a "chosen people," but is an honest attempt to get at universal values appropriate to mankind the world over, and at eternal values beyond the modes of governments and centuries, we must make clear our convictions first and then interpret them to any other inquirer. And we must find our brethren who are not classified as Brethren. We must be able to give reasons for the hope that is within us and must try honestly to understand any differing hope of any differing group of people. Also we must keep our convictions in their order of importance. Out of these attempts it may be that we shall find an opportunity for a greater testimony in this struggling, groping world.

Teaching Our Children the Ways of Peace

Whatever we adults are doing with our world, we want our children to live in nobler and better ways. We do not want them to be destroyers of lives and resources; we want them to live in peace.

Peacetime has some advantages for peace teaching, but wartime has advantages also. If we are determined, we can use war conditions to teach peace ways effectively.

Peace means a consistent way of living. We shall have to teach our children to live more consistently and effectively than we live. This requires many complex forces in their lives. The following are some of them:

1. An appropriate diet. Food makes a difference in disposition and outlook. "Tell me what you eat and I will tell you what you are."

2. A sense of security. This means a friendly atmosphere. Children are sensitive. In a hostile world they are worse off than the man without a country. In a warm home they grow heartily. It means also ways out of their fears. They need accurate information for honest questions, spurs to courageous action, and steady examples of confidence and goodwill. "Perfect love casteth out fear" [1 John 4:18, KJV]. Security includes also a feeling of justice. When a child does wrong, someone else must stand for the right. Otherwise the foundations are shaken for him. It means second chances. Forgiveness does not annihilate the past—it furnishes an antidote for it. The repentant bankrupt needs new credit to work with.

3. A wide range of interests, "a sign and a guard of sanity." War tends to shrink interests and warp the imagination. Shifting attention often from suffering and hardship to flowers, crops, and trees, to insects and birds, to clouds and stars, helps to make life not only tolerable, but triumphant.

4. A sense of destiny, directing and driving the life. Mrs. [Martin] Niemöller is said to have asked her sons their future vocations when their father was in prison already for not giving in to the Nazi regime. All said they were going to become ministers. Fred Richards felt last fall in his federal

Dan West, "Teaching Our Children the Ways of Peace," undated, Dan West Biographical File, Brethren Historical Library and Archives.

trial that he was carrying on the record of his father. Moses chose "rather to suffer affliction with the people of God than to enjoy the pleasures of sin for a season" [Heb. 11:25, KJV]. The heritage of the historic peace churches and others can be used to develop adventurous spirits in a great cause.

Here are some recommendations about what to do and what not to do. For background and indirect teaching, the following suggestions may be helpful:

1. Set the examples you want your children to follow. Otherwise "what you are talks so loudly I cannot hear what you say." Many deep beliefs are fixed before the child is five years old.

2. Make your home the most friendly place your child can find. There should be no boss there.

3. Make home chores habitual by making them satisfactory to your child.

4. Help him to big-muscle activity out-of-doors. It eases the strain better than small-muscle activity indoors. When possible, build many activities around the needs for food, clothing, and shelter.

5. Stress cooperative play. Competitive players in an orchestra do not make good music.

6. Teach habits of relaxation, and make naps habitual while the child is small. Strain and fatigue damage morale for peacemakers as well as or soldiers

7. Help the child to restrict his wants in a world of hunger. "Special privilege is the essence of immorality."

8. Cultivate his sense of humor. Smiling eases strain also.

9. Provide chances for him to know the children of other serious peacemakers. His "primary groups" will make or break him.

10. Make up the bulk of invited guests from underprivileged families and from adventurous spirits. Do not ask many of "the Joneses," and do not ask them often.

11. Make up for the hard blows to his spirit received at school and elsewhere, but guard against pity. Talk over unpleasant events to "get the terror out of them." Then touch the heroic in him.

12. Work to make your local church a friendly society which makes up for the lacks in other homes and elsewhere in your community.

These are suggestions for direct teaching:

1. Don't talk about the war. Talk rather about positive matters and good things to do, especially about those not yet done. "What gets your attention gets you."

2. Turn the radio away from war news. "Whatsoever things are true . . . honest . . . just . . . pure . . . lovely . . . of good report . . . think on these things" [Phil. 4:8, KJV]. The same will hold for newspapers. Maybe we should stop taking newspapers.

3. Read aloud and/or tell reliable stories of the heroes of peace. Save money elsewhere to provide materials for this. Avoid Bible stories about war for younger children.

4. Teach the child to hate, not people, but destructive customs and brutalizing forces, diseases, and injurious insects.

5. Shift his attention from instruments of war to the intended effects of those instruments, the destruction and suffering. Let him see the harm to those who use these instruments.

6. Help him to learn the techniques of settling his own quarrels.

7. Point out the best values in your neighborhood. If you can honestly do it, try to make your child proud of your community.

8. Teach the habits of self-reliance and cooperation both. "Every man shall bear his own burden" [Gal. 6:5, KJV]. "Bear ye one another's burden" [Gal. 6:2, KJV].

9. Furnish an antidote for personal ambition. Teach the meanings of *we, ours, us* more than of *I, mine, me.*

10. Avoid serious comparisons of children's abilities and characteristics.

11. Minimize grade marks in school. There are better motives for learning and for satisfaction.

12. Help the child to study geography sympathetically. Stress the people with different color, customs, and religions. Develop the desire for travel, beginning with the underprivileged locally.

13. Teach that all people are the children of God, that he is our Father.

14. Explain life, death, and danger in terms of cause and effect, but make clear that we understand only part of them. Teach your child to accept the universe with all its suffering.

15. Stretch your child's imagination toward the kind of world we ought to have, and put him to work to this end.

16. When your child has developed a firm trust in people, make him wise to propaganda and eager for the truth, both pleasant and unpleasant. "The truth shall make you free" [John 8:32, KJV].

17. Teach him to prize both organized government and organized religion, but to accept the domination of neither the church nor the state. Stress the value of the church now.

18. Teach the songs of peace, not the songs of war.

19. After the meanings are fairly clear, teach the scriptures that tell of the peace way of living, but not before the child understands them.

The Brethren Peace Testimony in 1950

"New occasions teach new duties," bring new problems, and put new tests to old convictions. The modern world is so different from that of 1900, so much more interdependent, and so torn by conflicting philosophies that many who want to follow the Christ feel confused, and helpless, and alone.

But eternal values do not change, even under all the stresses of an industrial civilization gone to seed, supersonic speed, atom bombs, and worse problems. And they will not change with any future development. Toward helping every member of the Church of the Brethren (and everyone else we can reach) to see clearly and to hold to eternal values, we offer this summary of some important statements from Annual Conference during the past seven years.

The Huntingdon Conference (1944) referred to earlier statements made in peacetime; one from Winona Lake (1935), "We believe that all war is sin . . . wrong for Christians to support or to engage in it . . . [and] incompatible with the spirit, example, and teachings of Jesus."

Another from Lawrence (1938), "Our supreme allegiance is to Christ. Today many Christians are finding themselves faced with a conflict between this allegiance and the demands of the state. . . . [In] such a conflict a Christian must be true to his faith."

Admitting our many past failures, we spoke thus, during the war: "Recognizing that these statements were more easily made then than now, we do in this 1944 Conference unequivocally reaffirm them as the historic peace conviction of the Church of the Brethren. . . . We believe it appropriate, therefore, to call the entire church to repentance . . . to be expressed in unfaltering effort to correct our past mistakes and prevent future war, or, if that once more proves impossible, to abstain from participation in it."

The Manchester Conference (1945) spoke thus: "Because our religion demands our supreme loyalty to God rather than to the state, we are unalterably opposed to the principle of conscription. . . . We want to bear our share of the burdens of our country, but we cannot follow blindly."

On conscription, thus: "If, in spite of its obvious lack of wisdom and of the traditional American spirit, this measure should be enacted, we,

Dan West, "The Brethren Peace Testimony in 1950," August 1, 1950, Dan West Biographical File, Brethren Historical Library and Archives.

the Church of the Brethren, recommend that our members who might be affected by such a program shall refuse military training and seek alternative civilian service."

At Wenatchee (1946) we went further: "In case Congress should enact a peacetime conscription bill, we are unwilling to administer any type of alternative service unless it be free from government dominance. . . . Where government is good, we support it gladly. Where it is bad, we strive to make it good by the processes of Christian democracy. We recognize disobedience to law as a matter of last resort in the strain between the freedom of conscience and the authority of the state."

At Orlando (1947) these words: "We reaffirm with deepest solemnity and commitment the historic peace position of the Brethren. We believe today that war and preparation for war are sinful and suicidal, contrary to the spirit and teaching of Jesus Christ. . . . [We] protest . . . the Truman policy of military aid to foreign nations to contain Russia . . . . In case universal military training is established by our government, we go on record as reaffirming the position on alternative service taken at the Wenatchee Conference in June 1946.

"We believe that our relations with Russia should be on the plane of the Good Samaritan . . . .

"We urge our young brethren and sisters to choose only those vocations which will contribute to creating, healing, serving, sharing, and witnessing; to stay out of all such vocations as would compromise their peace testimony in the event of another war."

At Colorado Springs (1948) we approved a special "Statement on Position and Practices of the Church of the Brethren in Relation to War," reaffirming the 1935 resolution (cited above), and denying the authority of the state to conscript citizens for military purposes against their convictions. Further, "As Christian citizens we consider it our duty to obey all civil laws which do not violate these higher laws (of God, D. W.). We seek, however, to go beyond the demands of law, giving time, effort, life, and property in a ministry to human needs without regard to race, creed, or nationality."

Recognizing the wide range of conscientious action (from refusing to register on to accepting full military service, and also constructive civilian service), "the church seeks to maintain a fellowship of all who sincerely follow the guidance of conscience. It does, however, recommend that as a matter of

Christian conviction and practice, its membership support the historic position of the church, namely—nonparticipation in military training and service and the war system, in general.

"[Our] members cannot consistently accept any service within the military forces or under military supervision. We commend to them instead a constructive alternative service under the direction of the church or some other civilian agency."

In its regular resolutions, the Colorado Springs Conference also said: "[We] reaffirm our conviction that all war is sinful, and that all attempts to promote and prepare for war are inimical to peace and antagonistic to Christ's way . . . . [We] register our protest . . . against the powerful propaganda from many agencies now being used to create fear, suspicion, and hatred of other countries, especially of Russia.

"We call upon our people and upon all our Christian brethren everywhere . . . to urge our government to explore and follow every possibility of peaceful discussion with Russia of the problems outstanding between us."

The Ocean Grove Conference (1949) spoke thus: "The times demand a church made up of committed Christians. We therefore call upon every member of our church to a commitment of his whole life—to spend his life only in a vocation to which he is called of God, and through which he can humbly serve his Christ, and share in the Kingdom He is establishing; to live simply and frugally that his soul may thrive and that he may share sacrificially; to dedicate money, land, time, and skills to the relief of hunger and suffering, to the work of the church, and the evangelization of the world.

"We urge our people to align themselves with those movements which work to make international organizations more effective, and to undergird them by developing our program of increasing the goodwill in the world."

This year at Grand Rapids the Conference resolved: "We know that men are making deadly weapons sufficient to destroy mankind, and against their use there is no protection but man's conscience and the providence of God. As Christians we realize that we are partly responsible for the lack of discernment of moral values in the world today, and we express penitence for our blindness and lack of courage. . . . We believe that we should fulfill our civic responsibility by supporting at the ballot box those measures which seem most in harmony with Christian principles, that for this reason we should let our representatives know that we are opposed to all unchristian measures such as atomic warfare, peacetime conscription, the manufacture of the hydrogen bomb, and the armament race, convinced that such measures are diametrically opposed to the moral law, and will lead to our destruction."

"We appeal to the church to remember its first task . . . to witness to the way of Christ . . . to take the message of redemption to the far places of the earth, and we must not fail in this crucial time."

Our people must know and understand the central conviction in all these statements. Some Brethren have never heard them; to such our duty is to inform and explain. Some have heard, and meant well, but waver under war propaganda; to them our duty is to remind, and to assure them that we mean to "make it stick," and fulfill the faith of our fathers. To the unconvinced, we must make the word flesh; some day that will convince them of the power of God and the way of God.

Brethren Service Commission
General Brotherhood Commission
22 South State Street
Elgin, Illinois

Some Implications of Pacifist Theory for Politics and International Relations

Christians are the most numerous and the most active—but not the most uni-fied "people of the Book," as some Hindus have characterized Jews, Christians, and Moslems. All Christians have so much in common that we should be much more nearly united on matters of life and witness. But we differ widely on the interpretation of Jesus' words, and on the "mind of Christ" [1 Cor. 2:16] in the New Testament and in the thinking of Christians for the last nineteen centuries. One historic difference has to do with the killing of our fellow men by intent. Most Christians are still willing to kill Christians on occasion—in war.

Evidently the early church had no problem here. For nearly two centuries not one Christian entered the Roman army, and not one soldier stayed in it after he became a Christian. Many conditions were different then, but that early record is consistent—and (I hold) might have remained so. However, Constantine and others introduced some far-reaching changes. From about AD 330 to 1937 the majority of Christians did not accept the *possibility* of anyone being a pacifist and a Christian. At the Oxford Conference (1937) it was agreed generally that such might be possible.

But sincere Christians have become increasingly uneasy about the war problem. One of the earlier efforts was the exemption of priests, when there was only one Christian church, from military duty. So far so good.

However, small groups (including the Waldensians, who followed the early French Christians and never united with the Roman Church) have carried the idea farther—no member of the Christian group was to go to war. The historic peace churches are inheritors of that tradition and have devel-oped it somewhat. And we are responsible for its further development, if we are willing to carry the burden.

But there are other difficult problems where the Brethren, Friends, and Mennonites differ also. There is a cluster of hard ones centering about the matter of government, all the way from local school boards to those of inter-

Dan West, "Some Implications of Pacifist Theory for Politics and International Relations," May 22, 1954, box 50, Dan West Papers, Brethren Historical Library and Archives.

national tariffs, armies, policies, etc. We are not anarchists; we all accept the principle of government, at least within our own groups. But we have varied on matters of government in wider community groups.

So long as we lived in relative isolation from other peoples (either geographically or culturally), it was a fairly easy problem. Then each group could maintain its own culture. But communities came closer—our lives were more intertwined with the lives of people with other faiths and practices—and pressures became heavier. These factors brought newer, harder problems. The old solutions were no longer adequate; and the old cultures are now uncertain. And so—

Some Important Problems

1. Can the historic peace churches maintain the historic faith during the Hydrogen Age?

2. Is war wrong for all Christians—and for other people too?

3. Do we have any further obligations to the people of our age?

Yes is my answer to all three questions. It is only one man's conviction, but it is clear after about forty years of searching. Brethren, Friends, and Mennonites will differ (both as persons and as groups) on some phases of all of these questions; but the differences are not of the most importance. We ought to be impelled by our Christian faith as we are being compelled by modern experience to make clear the reasons for the hope that is within us. If we share what we deeply believe in Christian fellowship we shall all profit—whatever the outcome of the cooperative search. My conviction is offered in humility but without any apology. I hope that any who differ from me will approach the problems in the same way.

Now the same questions in more detail:

1. We are more likely to lose our historic faith now than ever before. With the odds against us, I hold that we must maintain that faith at all costs—and they may be very high. But to maintain it we must fulfill it. The light of God which has come to us cannot be put under a bushel. We cannot keep our faith by refrigeration. The little chick cannot return to the eggshell. We have put our hands to the plow, and dare not turn back. We are committed to Christ and his kingdom on earth—a dynamic kingdom in a changing world.

2. War is wrong for all Christians—and for everybody else because Christ is our standard for measuring life. "There is no Christian way to kill a man." So spoke representatives of Brethren, Friends, and Mennonites to the Methodist bishops in 1936. It is still our firm faith however short our practice may be. That concept is working deeper into the hearts of more Christians than ever before. If we are statesmen of the spirit, we shall witness now better than we have ever done before.

No easy task this. The intricate life of the modern world, the speedy changes in well-established cultures and the forming of new ones, the clamor for worldly wisdom as the only real wisdom—the "confusion of tongues" on the relationship between love and justice—the current blight of distrust in American life and between national groups—these and other factors make this problem harder than ever before.

3. We must carry our expanding social obligations within the Christian church and outside it. We *are* our brothers' keepers, too. Both our survival as groups and the survival of our Christian culture in the larger sense demand that we tell our story by word and deed wherever we can earn a hearing. Small size may be a handicap, but it can be an asset, too. "To whom much has been given of him much shall be required." That means us now—never mind the size.

When the Friends withdrew from the Pennsylvania legislature after repeated efforts to carry on the Holy Experiment, the policy of Pennsylvania became as warlike as that of other colonies. That story may become a parable of the world in the twentieth century.

As persons and groups we may vary in our answers to all three questions. But it is likely that the third one will give us the most trouble and we may differ more there. Let us look at it a bit more closely—

Human Nature

Is there any reasonable hope for an effective hearing? If not, our social responsibilities may be less. Many Christians in both millennia have had a low estimate of the mine-run of human nature. The recurrent view (now the dominant, current view again) holds that man is evil, and naturally so, since the sin of Adam and Eve. And this scripture is often referred to as final: "Behold, I was shapen in iniquity; and in sin did my mother conceive me" [Psalm 51:5, KJV]. Granting that it may have been true in that case—nobody really knows—I get the suggestion that David offered this slander on his mother as a rationalization of his own sin. Anyhow no extenuating circumstances were allowed when the prophet Nathan spoke to him. All of us accept the fact of sin, among Christians too. But what of the sinner—does he *have* to stay that way?

Too ignorant for dogmatic speaking (I'd like to ask questions of anyone who *is* sure) and too close to the picture for any final judgment of the current emphasis on the alleged evil nature of man, I am quite willing to hazard a guess: The latest style in theological thinking has been unduly influenced by the mounting frustrations of our modern life on sensitive souls. If this sorry view is taken at par by the historic peace churches, we shall lose our hope for the future, as well as our witness for some basic teachings of our Christ. And we shall lose our own youth to some lesser philosophy, maybe to one not at all Christian. If we deeply believe that the gospel of God will not work with the erring children of God, we are licked already. Somebody else was more hopeful: "My word . . . shall not return unto me void" [Isaiah 55:11, KJV]. If God still loves the world he must have hopes for his people. And if that is so, we have sufficient reason that our wholehearted witness will be effective—someday if not in our time.

We have the word of Jesus that there is none good but God. But that idea is different from the one that all human beings are essentially evil. At a time of deep frustration [Jesus] discriminated better than some theologians do now: "The spirit indeed is willing, but the flesh is weak" [Matt. 26:41, KJV]. Don't we know that well enough from our own experience?

Even that weak flesh has heroic possibilities, and in the direction of our historic faith. Witness the transcending of narrow state loyalties by the American forefathers when they determined to form a "more perfect union." Witness also in our own time the rising of the people of India to independence, with chief reliance on nonviolent political activity and "soul-force." These rate events indicate that human nature has potentialities far beyond what the current theological view allows.

But our main task reaches far beyond what people believe about theological matters. It is primarily other—in the field of action. What we do is more important than how we think.

Three More Hard Problems

If we take seriously any fuller responsibility for our fellowmen (there are 2.4 billion of them, and the number is increasing rapidly), the following problems need careful scrutiny and some new experimentation, looking toward their solution:

1. What is our basic relation to the world with which our faith puts us always at tension?

2. What is our attitude to government in our communities—local through international?

3. Where do we draw the line in the relative series of efforts to change people?

Let us look at these problems in greater detail:

1. There are at least six recognized historic positions possible to take in relation to our world, with a case possible to be made for every one of them:

   a. Withdrawal from the world because of the evil in it—a kind of monasticism.

   b. Identification with our world—acceptance of realities, and "adjustment" to them.

   c. Vocational dualism. "Holy men" don't participate in the evil world; others do.

   d. Private–public dualism. "My heart belongs to God; my body, to the state" ([Martin] Luther).

   e. Personal discipleship. We belong to Christ; and so—no compromise with evil. We refuse it, but do not run away from it.

   f. Transformationism—to redeem as much of life as possible where things are mixed up.

Some choice here is necessary for every Christian. And whatever choice is made is very far-reaching. My own choice is a combination of *e* and *f*, with a leaning toward *e* where both values cannot be integrated. It would be illuminating to know your choice here, too; and it would be very good to learn the resultant choices of Brethren, of Friends, and of Mennonites.

A helpful, though imperfect analogy to my position appears in Arthur Morgan's little book published in 1936, *The Long Road*:

The few exceptionally productive cattle of half a century ago, if they had been scattered through the entire mass of the cattle population and had been bred indiscriminatingly, would soon have been swallowed up and their distinctive quality lost by continued dilution in the great mass of low quality, as was the case with high bred cattle supplied by the Great Northern Railroad (in Minnesota). It was because the professional breeder carefully kept his herd distinct, and constantly made more exacting standards for membership in his herds, that the slowly achieved qualities of his best stock were perpetuated, and made available wherever a desire for improvement existed. . . .

As compared with the simple and limited aims of any breeder of thoroughbred animals, the purposes of distinctive social groups . . . are exceedingly complex and elusive. If groups of men and women are to undertake exceptionally clear and exacting definition of those personal and social qualities that would be desirable in any form of society, and are to commit themselves to living uncompromisingly by those standards, then they should take precautions both against provincialism and against softness. . . .

If such men are to escape the constant dilution of their purposes by society at large, it is desirable that there be *islands of brotherhood* where men of like purposes can strengthen each other and can create a milieu in accordance with the universal expedients of a good life. . . .

The social order in which we must come to feel at home may be likened to the life of a seagull, forever in the ceaselessly changing, moving elements of sea and air, ever ready instantly to adjust itself to wind or wave. . . . When I speak of . . . communities of like-minded and like-spirited people, it is not in the attitude of proposing retreat from the currents of the times.

Here again Brethren, Friends, and Mennonites will differ, both as persons and as groups. It seems to me that the Mennonites have done better than the rest of us in maintaining islands of brotherhood—hard as that is now. Also the Friends have done better than the rest of us in avoiding provincialism— hard as that is for people who are different. I should like to see *all of us* achieve *both* values in a better way than has ever been done. Here the Brethren may have an advantage, if we can re-earn our self-respect as fast as we widen our sympathies—and that seems the hardest task of all.

2. Our basic relation to government can be illustrated by another figure—

A good hotel has guests; and it has a manager. Also, it has an owner or a group of stockholders who own it. But the functions are different. The guests have no responsibility for each other; and they don't make the rules—they abide by them or move out. The manager has definite responsibility for both hotel and rules; he is responsible to the owners.

Speaking now without more than crude approximation as to time and place—Mennonites (at least one important group of them) are guests in the hotel, good guests, who obey the rules. But the hotel is distinctly not their home. They have no real home anywhere. They are pilgrims and sojourners. The Friends (at least one important group of them) live there too as guests, but they own the place, at least in part. They are good guests, but they are responsible for more than themselves. They look the rules over critically. If the management or the rules are unsatisfactory, it is their job to do everything in keeping with their culture to change one or both—whether they are in the minority or majority. The status of the Brethren in this hotel figure is not so clear.

Now for the interpretation—

The extreme Mennonite position approaches zero in matters of citizenship except in local communities. That of the Friends—extreme—approaches 100 percent *without accepting anyone else's standards.* (In contrast, another widely different group of Christians accepts 100 percent citizenship also; but their motto is "My country, right or wrong.") The extreme Mennonites have no concern beyond how the policy affects *them.* One spoke thus before the Hydrogen Age: "We think the hotel is going to burn down."

Brethren don't agree here, and we are harder to classify—a little like the Irishman's flea: "You put your finger on him and he ain't there!" We have had something of a sliding scale between these two extremes. In colonial life we were moving toward fuller citizenship. In the nineteenth century we had little responsibility for government, almost zero in the scale. Now we are moving back again, especially since World War I. It is regrettable that we have usually "adjusted" more than we have taken responsibility for changing government policy of officials. Incidentally, the poor quality of Indiana politics, where Brethren, Friends, and Mennonites are thick, is a heavy commentary on the civic responsibility of *all* of us. If any group of us determines to put the laws of God first and then take hold of the hard problems of government, we can hold to fuller citizenship without spiritual loss. Otherwise we become acculturated, and lose our savor. Brethren future policy is unsettled. The Bluffton Conference ought to help make it clear. I believe we should have a strong "spring" pushing us steadily toward fuller citizenship responsibilities: But it ought to "give" when conditions change; it should not be rigid.

3. Some problems in relativity. "If white is good, and black is bad, All of my friends are gray or plaid."

The idea of relativity is rough on persons who grew up accustomed to thinking in terms of only black and white. But we can learn to discriminate between grays—and to get beyond the lesser relativities. We accept the relativity of color in the rainbow; that idea may be useful here also. Where we "get off" on the scale of varied social "pressures" is a necessary but difficult and often painful decision. The following chart [on the next page] by [Cecil John] Cadoux from *Christian Pacifism Re-examined* may be helpful to see some of our differences and through that some basic values: "[The tabular statement] is not intended to furnish an exact . . . classification . . . but only to illustrate . . . the broad lines of [the types of pressure]."

All persons and groups are in this series somewhere—nobody is left out. But nobody in Christendom would accept as valid the three items, 29, 30, and 31—without renouncing his essential faith in Christ. We are past that sort of thing, unless we revert. At the other end of the series likely all of us would take in more than items 1, 2, and 3. Maybe most Mennonites would go as far as 10 if 7, 8, and 9 were skipped. Maybe most Friends would go as far as 22, after omitting 13. Our Master displayed anger (item 18) on several occasions; the 23rd chapter of Matthew is really rough on the scribes and Pharisees.

Most Brethren have varied on both sides of 14, would exclude 13, and— (maybe because we like to eat too well)—we would not take easily to item 8 (collective). We need to be clear on what we would favor doing and not doing in this series; for example, we have no clear policy on strikes or civil disobedience. And others need to be settled, too. I guess the Friends and Mennonites have some unfinished business here also. And all of us may well take several

TABULAR STATEMENT OF METHODS OF PRESSURE

Category	No.	General and Individual	Collective
Noncoercive (influence, etc.)	1	Force of example	
	2	Quasi-magnetic power	
	3	Intercessory prayer	
	4	Telepathy	
	5	Kindness, trust, forgiveness, and "nonresistance"	Passive resistance to persecution, etc.
	6	Display of unsought suffering	The "martyr-nation"
	7	Obtrusion of self-inflicted suffering (e.g., personal hunger strike)	
	8	Scenic displays	The collective hunger strike
	9	Spoken or written arguments and appeals	Processions
	10	Promises	"Leaflets," petitions
	11	Rewards	
	12	Bribes	
Coercive — Non-injurious — Psychological	13	Refusal to cooperate	
	14	Disobedience to orders	Voting
	15	Threats	Active resistance to persecution, etc. Strike, boycott.
	16	Anger	
Coercive — Non-injurious — Physical	17	Mild punishment as a part of home discipline	"The War of Nerves"
	18	Restraining a violent individual	School-discipline
Coercive — Injurious	19	Knocking a bully down	
	20	Cruel or over-severe punishment	Humane police-administration
	21	Violent assault	Mild imprisonment
	22	Casual or incidental homicide	The police truncheon
	23	Torture	"Do-the-boys' Hall"
	24	Mutilation	Prolonged imprisonment
	25	Willful murder	The cat
	26		Capital punishment
	27		Armed rebellion
	28		War
	29		Mediaeval persecution
	30		Oriental penalties
	31		Gratuitous massacre

looks at our relation to the modern world in general, and to governments in particular.

A Suggested Policy for the Historic Peace Churches

As war becomes more nearly totalitarian, peace efforts must become more integrated. But our faith should develop our spiritual integrity faster than social necessity compels action. With no real hiding place from the problems of war (Costa Rica and Paraguay may be so only temporarily), we cannot dodge either the growing threat to our faith or our responsibility for the world as well as ourselves We are becoming our brothers' keepers more than ever before. The recent advertisement in the *New York Times* is a recognition of that fact.

Our basic problems of what to do in a complex, suffering, warring, changing world is a big one. Here are three main phases of it:

1. Relief and rehabilitation of war sufferers, and those who suffer from chronic social ills.

2. Opposition to both actual war and its causes—an unqualified NO.

3. Positive peacemaking—an unqualified YES.

These spelled out might look somewhat thus:

1. Across the centuries we have accepted responsibility for suffering humanity after war and the natural calamities, at least in small ways. In modern times from the adventurous beginnings by the Friends in 1917, we have attempted bigger jobs and with steadier purpose. Within five days after the armistice in November 1918, some Friends were in Berlin, Germany, offering to help. The work they did had far-reaching effects—true, not far enough, but better than what anyone else did; and it earned a remarkable goodwill in wider areas. Mennonites have done some commendable work in Korea within the past year. Brethren "motors" were a bit slower in starting, but once we got going we helped more on this great task than ever before in our history. If our three groups could find a formula for closer cooperation as well as our spiritual forefathers did in colonial history, we could offer a much better witness. Someday we shall do that, and more.

Good deeds sometimes have quick political effects. An interesting story illustrates this in the wake of a natural calamity. A small tornado swept through Goshen, Indiana, in March 1942, killing two persons and destroying much property. The next morning there was an offer of Mennonite CPS

[Civilian Public Service] men to clean up. But the Red Cross official was not kindly disposed toward such action. However, when nobody else was available, public opinion moved the Red Cross and the city council to accept the proposition. The boys came in and did a good job. Some weeks later Congressman Grant of our district asked me in Washington whether Frank Ebersole (a Mennonite) would make a good mayor for Goshen. I could not say as I did not know him. He became the next mayor, from 1943 to 1947. What if that would be a parable of many situations in our war-torn world?

On the other hand, we cannot often expect quick or easy political effects of good deeds. The excellent child feeding program of the Friends in Germany did not prevent the same persons from accepting the Nazi pattern half a generation later.

2. If we insist that we are opposed to war, we are committed both logically and spiritually to oppose the effects and causes of war, as well as participation in it. And all of them are hard to oppose, since we are so closely tied in with our modern world. We do make compromises. Minor compromises should be made cheerfully. Major compromises *never*. What is major, what minor, is another important decision. Here are two of mine: I carry a registration card, and I pay federal taxes. But if we stutter in our witness—or just keep silent— that witness fades. And if our mouths are stopped by special consideration for CO's, we become even greater accomplices in the evils of the draft system. The less we do to oppose war at all points, the greater the case our neoorthodox brethren can make against us—we are shedding part of our responsibility. We who accept the rightness of spiritual warfare must "keep in contact with the enemy"—not against flesh and blood, but against cussedness in high places, etc.

Suppose we had another chance at the 1930s with the perspective we have now—maybe before the Newton Conference of 1935, but certainly after it—we would have supported wholeheartedly the National Council for the Prevention of War; its purposes were right and some of those insights were valid. So was the aim of the Emergency Peace Campaign right even if some of its methods were open to question. We would have done a better job in Spain, and elsewhere, and it might not have been too late even in 1937. Maybe there was not enough of "the spiritual stuff out of which international law is made" (John Brierly, of Cambridge University). But maybe there were just not enough deeply concerned persons at the grass roots, or at top levels of government—not enough George Lansburys, or Toyohiko Kagawas, or [E.] Stanley

Joneses, or [Saburo] Kurusus and others. Maybe there were both of these lacks and others. But certainly we could have worked further upstream than we did. We could have furnished a number of persons of the right caliber—had we seen what we see now, and had we cared as we ought to care now. World War II was not as easily put over on the American people as was World War I. And maybe it will be harder to sell any "World War III."

If we had been working steadily on this problem before the threat of the draft law of 1940 made us work to save our own youth from war activities, we would have done a better job than we were able to do in CPS.

But there is no use in crying over spilled milk. Here are the 1950s and this is the Hydrogen Age. What might we do if we would be aware, in local churches and communities and at Bluffton—and if we were as deeply concerned as our faith ought to make us? Even at this late date, if the historic peace churches would appeal to all American Christians first and then all other Christians wholeheartedly to renounce war and its preparations because it is unchristian, that might mean an effective turning of the tide which now moves the world toward a war that may mean annihilation of most of the human race. A clear NO might be more effective than it ever was before.

3. But NO is never an adequate answer. Opposition to war or to its causes is never sufficient. A world can never be built on negations—even negations of evil. The empty house is always a dangerous situation, we have evidence that enemies of our faith are ready to take advantage of any kind of vacuum: economic, ideational, or spiritual. We must develop a stronger YES than our strongest NO.

We have the makings of a better YES than we have ever given. Some think that we have better makings of YES than anybody else. Back in 1941 Arthur Holt of Chicago spoke out of history and predicted thus:

> A century ago the leadership of Protestant America was in the hands of the theologians. Later it came to the revivalists. Now it is coming to the historic peace churches. The older leaders led with the jaw. These lead with the hand.

There are many new possibilities:

a. Here is one in the economic field: Back in 1951 three outstanding economists from the historic peace churches ([Quaker] Kenneth Boulding, [Brethren] Earl Garver, and [Mennonite] Carl Kreider) met with a small group of patternmakers in the State Department on the problem of reconversion to a peacetime economy after the armament spree would be over. The government officials seemed to have no well-considered plan then—nor now. That was a small beginning, though a big opportunity. Because we have no plan either we can remain humble.

Another possibility for creative adventure is in the field of economic life for homes and churches If we see far enough we will discern how much we are tied in with the war-producing system. And we are in increasing danger of succumbing to the temptations of "war prosperity." During the 1940s when Mennonites had paid three-quarters of a million dollars to support CPS, one Mennonite leader told me that this figure may have been less than 25 percent of what Mennonites had already made out of the war. My own guess is that Brethren and Friends have an even less complimentary record than that. With our kind of Christian faith, we cannot consistently take—or keep—"blood money" (the extra purchasing power from war activity)! Maybe we ought to be giving ten times as much as we are now giving to help a needy world. That would be a witness that even cynical critics would respect. "Politics is economics, and economics is politics. And both are ethics."

b. In the intellectual field we might become much more creative also. I believe we have possibilities in our cultures which, once made articulate, would give something (out of both old and new elements) worthy of export. And the human mind must have some ideas to hang on to. If less responsible persons or groups catch the attention of the world's increasing millions of people, dangerous ideas will take root and grow. "Human nature tends to accept whatever is presented to it effectively." The Nazis played on this theme with no regard for the truth. What might we be able to get across if we were determined to tell the truth we know—even when it cuts across customary thinking?

Here again we can be learners. Looking backward it is regrettable that our workers in India did not always make clear our peace testimony, nor work for land reform, nor for independence. They left those matters to non-Christian leaders. With a chance at better insight we can learn and do better. Here in America we can support the Friends Committee on National Legislation, and help furnish content for Frank Laubach's world literacy program—to cite two examples.

Following is a testimony from a surprising source: Some years ago [Field Marshal] Jan Smuts was the South African delegate to UN. One day he and [Andrew] W. Cordier were discussing [Hartley] Shawcross, the British delegate. Smuts inquired, "Isn't he a Quaker?" Cordier did not know. "I believe he is," Smuts went on. "Anyhow he comes from Quaker background." Then the old warrior-empire builder-philosopher became very thoughtful; and he continued: "Humanity is very tired of war. It has lost the way. And the Quakers know that way. Someday we shall have to come to the Quaker philosophy for the basis of our political decisions."

c. We believe in prayer—maybe not so much as we claim. I am coming to believe that it is the mightiest force in the world, still unused for the most part. If the members of the historic peace churches would live first and then pray as one committed man—not only for the "peace of Jerusalem" [Psalm 122:6, KJV] but for the *shalom* of the whole world, I am convinced that new power would be released—maybe enough to turn the tide in our time. Whatever the immediate results, it belongs to our timeless job because it fits with God's will. "The effectual fervent prayer of a righteous man availeth much" [James 5:16, KJV]. What could the prayers of righteous Brethren, Friends, and Mennonites do if steady, wholehearted, and unified?

d. If we try good things and fail, or are misunderstood in our efforts we shall have to take suffering. But our essential job is still the same, whether we succeed soon or late. And there is nothing essentially new about suffering in our kind of world. All of us have been kicked around enough not to expect easier lives than our forefathers had—if we are as determined as they were. And our children ought to be taught the essentials of healthy suffering—not too much "adjustment" to the world as we find it—until weak, floundering persons and groups learn better ways of responding. The rule of the cross is as real as the law of gravitation. And we are commanded to carry our crosses— not to worship his.

We must hold on to our relief and rehabilitation work—in fact, expand them. Also, we must develop a more effective opposition to the whole war system. But more than either of those we must take new responsibility as peacemakers, furnishing all we can of the moral, intellectual, social, and spiritual equivalents of war. "Into the vicious circle we must introduce the redemptive spiral" (Kenneth Boulding).

Our Future Role—or Roles

With our small numbers we cannot hope to be effective REAGENTS for any big NO or any big YES. But we are not too small to serve as effective CATA-LYSTS in the sensitive chemistry of the mind, and in social life.

Changing to another figure, these words of Galen Barkdoll, a Dunker farmer-preacher, are worth pondering:

> The condenser on a 120-HP is a very small accessory but the 120-HP engine is very dependent on the tiny condenser. Gandhi focused the issues confronting his nation and his time in himself. He was the condenser. . . . Some Christian group must be the condenser in which the needed controls become effective. . . . Essential to such action (calling on UN to handle this scientific madness of nuclear weapon displays) is the initial sponsorship of some condenser group to:
>
> 1. collect what has been done and said in protest against nuclear warfare,
>
> 2. increase this protest internationally,
>
> 3. inform the world that its Christian conscience has been left responsible for the needed "spiritual controls," and
>
> 4. make it definitely apparent that a Merchants of Death revival is imminent unless controls are agreed upon and accepted. . . .
>
> If you know of anyone or group sufficiently concerned to be the condenser for this responsibility, please urge them . . . .

Maybe a third figure will be helpful: Along in 1945 Archibald MacLeish wrote somewhat thus: "We now accept the miracle of the atom, but we do not accept the miracle of the human heart." If even a handful of the members of the historic peace churches believe that the latter miracle is within the will of God, they can furnish a disproportionate share of the formula for the *chain reaction of the spirit.*

Some Things Have Been Done

In recent centuries, especially the last, new discoveries and inventions in human relations have been made; maybe some new values have been developed. And the historic peace churches have helped in the development—in homes, schools, prisons, mental hospitals, factories, etc.

Less than a century ago it was customary in many schools for Christian teachers to assume that pupils were hostile beings to be mastered. Even in some homes the same attitude prevailed: Only thirty years ago one fine husky German boy in Hammond, Indiana, told me: "My father beats me once in a while . . . but I don't mind it anymore," he added quickly and kindly. Parents and teachers are still floundering, and some have gone off the other side of the road, but gradually we are learning how to combine righteousness and love in homes and schools. That is hopeful for education in the future.

Beginning some centuries ago with Quakers who had reason to dislike prison conditions, we are learning to trust prisoners better—and to find them responding to that trust. Fanny [French] Morse at Hudson Training School for Girls half a century ago; Warden [Lewis] Lawes and Mrs. [Kathryn] Lawes at Sing Sing twenty years ago helped on that too. Less than fifteen years ago Kurt Lewin, Father [Edward] Flanagan, and others proved that unruly boys responded to trust in surprising ways. One of the fine developments of CPS was a new interest and new techniques in treating mental patients as persons. How far the results of that effort will go nobody knows.

Some businessmen are learning out of experience that just ordinary folks produce more in factories and are happier about it when treated with good-will. Charles McCormick of Baltimore, Jewel Tea Company of Chicago, General Electric Company of many places, are a few of them. Mary Follett tested some of the same values in Boston and New York more than thirty years ago. The evidence is piling up toward a justifiable conclusion: Our historic faith will work in more situations than we ourselves once believed. Now is it fair to project farther and into governmental patterns and try to have our faith expressed through *law, justice, and righteousness* as well as through mercy and love? Here we enter the field of politics. I believe it is possible, but not at all easy; instead it is a most difficult engineering feat.

Some Unfinished Business

Will love work in situations where policemen are on duty? In state legislatures? In Congress with persons like Senator [Joseph] McCarthy? In the UN Assembly in the offices and in the corridors outside? At conferences like those at Berlin, Caracas, and Geneva?

But before we church folks get to feeling superior and ready to give glib answers, let us ask a few more questions: Will love work in committee meetings, in church councils, in staff and faculty meetings and other places where we live intensely? Will our churches go as far in practice as the Supreme Court has ruled on segregation of Negroes in schools? And—how much more responsibility for government will we take in our new world? These are not academic questions—but real ones. It is in our field to try to answer them.

How Much Can We Do Together?

It would be good to have a statement on what the historic peace churches can say together. But maybe no one person can outline that—yet. A little dubious about even the most brilliant statements detached from active programs—"We integrate on the motor level better than we do on the verbal level" (Mary Follett), I would offer some concrete suggestions aimed at harnessing our faith to some of the political problems of our time. And maybe Brethren, Friends, and Mennonites can work together in new and old ways—once we come to feel that we need one another. I am not concerned about any structural union here, but I do feel that we need new patterns of hearty cooperation. Newton furnished one in 1935. Bluffton may furnish another in 1954. Here are some possibilities:

A. *Immediately*—1954 may not be too late.

1. Basing plans on the beginning we have made in the *New York Times* advertisement we can appeal strongly and steadily for the churches in America—all of them, including Catholics—to "choose the cross of Christ (instead of) the cross of hydrogen (and) be done with these fearful weapons . . ." (etc.). And we keep at it like the importunate widow.

2. From the Bluffton Conference we can appeal to the World Council of Churches at Evanston and to the pope to refuse to bless any kind of war in the future. We may fail the first time or the twentieth, but once we have done what we can, we may leave further responsibility to God and to our fellow Christians. There comes a subtle temptation—we hide behind our unofficial status as an excuse for doing nothing but talking to ourselves. Should that happen, Bluffton cannot become prophetic. If the representatives of our church groups come to one mind, of one accord, it will have a profound effect on all of our churches at their next meetings, whether it influences Evanston or not.

3. We can appeal as a body to the Congress of the United States and to the UN Assembly for immediate work toward disarmament.

4. We can ask our people to counsel in kindly, deeply concerned ways with senators and congressmen at home and at Washington. These are the persons who may have to vote for peace or for war within a few years' time—maybe within weeks or months.

5. We can attempt the "George Lansbury task" on a world scale. Appealing personally to the heads of fourteen governments for a change of policy in 1936 and 1937, he got a respectful hearing from most of them, including Hitler and [Benito] Mussolini, a fair hearing from Franklin Roosevelt, but none at all from the British government. (I got this story in 1938 from him in London.) Friends may be in a position to appeal in Russia now; with the backing of the rest of us they might be more effective. And all three groups are likely in a good position to appeal in the USA. Certainly a united appeal would get a better hearing.

Items 6, 7, 8, etc., can be added if we want to do more than these things, together.

Alfred Korzybski's warning may be appropriate to us, also: "If those who know why and how neglect to act, those who do not know will act, and the world will continue to flounder."

B. *Long-Term Possibilities*—no matter what happens to immediate plans.

1. We can try in better ways to guide our youth to better goals than to make money and to try to climb up in the world. Those biting words from Robert Louis Stevenson years ago and speaking of another country still apply in some situations: "The chief aim in education is to show us how we can serve both God and mammon." But we grown-ups will have to set better examples if we expect our youth to believe that we are wholeheartedly striving to serve only God when we have to deal with mammon, too.

2. We can pick up our reconstruction plans and training at Goshen, Manchester, and Haverford Colleges, blasted by the Starnes Amendment in 1943. The Haverford [Social and] Technical Assistance training program might furnish the nucleus of a greatly expanded program of nongovernmental assistance—(and maybe governmental, if our witness is not too heavily clouded)—to the needy around the world. If we are honest, we must recognize that nongovernmental activities often give a clouded witness, too.

3. We can furnish a goodly share of manpower and some of the content for the World Literacy Program sponsored by Frank Laubach and others.

4. We can support direct rehabilitation projects, such as the Heifer Project, CROP, etc.

5. We can sponsor in local communities visitors from other lands, creating between common people here and common people there (not governments) "the spiritual stuff out of which international law is made."

6. We can request the help of our ablest members in research and experiment in harnessing our faith to the hardest problems of world life. The Mormons know how to do this for their purposes. For more than eleven years I have dreamed that the historic peace churches might someday be known as the group that banished two old scourges of civilization—hookworm and malaria—to cite one possibility.

7. We can ask our people to give unstinting support, creative help, and kindly criticism to the Friends Committee on National Legislation. This steady, noncoercive kind of lobbying helps lawmakers to make up their minds; often they are puzzled as to what is the best possible thing to do—not seeing any "right" course of action.

8. We can offer to the US State Department and other governmental agencies our best help on their hard problems: economic, educational, spiritual. We could ask our best economists, our best educators, our best spiritual guides to work together and offer help wherever it is needed. One example, Elton Trueblood has a hard job; if he has to carry it without our help, it may be too much.

9. We can send committed Christian members into government and other kinds of service as needy areas for the expression of their Christian vocation. Yes, there are heavy risks, just as everywhere else. And *there must be places for getting off*—even at high cost; otherwise the casualty to our cause is not compensated by any great gain in public service. Some persons have been able to handle this difficult role well. Following are some examples within the past century of both "success" and "failure" in high places:

   a. John Bright, as prime minister of England in 1864 when "England was tired of peace," opposed the mounting Crimean War while in office. But he failed.

   b. John Hay, Secretary of State, about 1900, worked to turn the Boxer Indemnity toward the education of Chinese students here in the USA. He succeeded.

c. William Jennings Bryan in 1916 resigned from the office of Secretary of State when he saw the USA moving toward World War I. He failed.

d. Charles Evans Hughes, while Secretary of State, startled the Washington Naval Conference (1922) with a new formula functioning toward peace. (We were near war with England then.) He succeeded.

e. [Elizabeth Cutter] Morrow (wife of the ambassador from the USA) helped to turn the tide against a war with Mexico in 1927. She invited Will Rogers and Charles Lindbergh to make a goodwill tour. She succeeded—the countries have been more friendly since.

f. George Lansbury might have become prime minister of England if he had given up his pacifism during the Spanish Civil War. Instead he resigned as chairman of the British Labor Party. A failure, seen from worldly eyes.

g. Jeannette Rankin voted in Congress against war with Japan the day after Pearl Harbor—the only vote against that war. Her "failure" will someday be reviewed as statesmanship.

Items 10, 11, 12, etc., can be added if we want to do more.

We have no real chance to be neutral in this kind of world. And we will make many compromises. There are two great dangers:

- We shall not recognize some of the compromises we actually make, or

- We shall not discriminate well between major and minor compromises. We may become pharisaical if someone else makes a different one; or we may become dull—rationalizing our own as "the greatest good to the greatest number," or we may try for the "lesser of two evils."

As I see it, our great obligation is not to any doctrinaire simon-pure consistency. But we are under deep obligation to *"hunger and thirst after righteousness"* [Matt. 5:6, KJV]—*the righteousness of God*, beyond all of our relativities—and to test all of our compromises in the light of God's will. There must be an unmistakable integrity in all we try to do, as we try to give our maximum witness.

C. *For Both Immediate and Long-Term*—whatever happens.

We can pray steadily, earnestly for peace. The example of the junior class in history at the Taft High School, Chicago, is a good cue from the next generation; belonging to many different churches they take time out at the beginning of every day to pray for peace on earth. One boy prays, "That we may all live together as one family."

- - - - -

Brethren, Friends, and Mennonites need one another as never before; and we need the help of all other Christians. We need to work on any organizational union now, but we do need better patterns of cooperation. If we learn those better patterns soon enough, we may serve as important channels for God's miracle for the world—all the while remembering that he has other channels too. The big problem at the UN is national sovereignty; maybe our big problem is church sovereignty. But that can be solved once we become members one of another as we come to belong more wholeheartedly to the body of Christ.

We have come to the kingdom for such a time as this. Together we can do much better and much more than any one of us, or all of us, working only separately.

Peace Education in Homes

WHAT IT TAKES

Two fathers were enjoying a long friendly discussion in a home. Their main thought was the peace question. The guest was much stronger for the declared position of the church than was the host; but both were searching honestly. Finally the host gave this strange prediction: "Well, thirty years from now my son will be a peace leader in the church, while yours will be an admiral in the Navy."

That stuck in the guest's mind. Was the host correct in this kind of prediction? Even after long patient efforts on basic education for peace, would parents have to fail? Would their son leave it when it came time for him to decide? Solomon thought, "Train up a child in the way he should go, and when he is old he will not depart from it" [Prov. 22:6]. But maybe Solomon was wrong here.

Before making any final decision it may be well to look at the setting for peace education in modern America. Not only does USA have enough bombs of various kinds to blast any other great power off the face of the earth, but there are plans to develop a "military culture."

Before the latest White House Conference on Childhood and Youth (1950) a survey had been made of the attitudes of children toward war and related subjects. It showed that the children were not much concerned about it. Some other studies showed that such a person is much disturbed emotionally when he is put into the armed forces upon graduation from high school—so much so that it was concluded that a healthy personality cannot be developed thus. The remedy proposed was the development of a "military culture" in America over the next twenty-five to fifty years, beginning with plans for getting children in the first grade to use war words in their vocabularies. The same plan followed through would make them slide easily into a war pattern upon finishing the twelfth grade.

It seems that the plans are developing gradually in this direction. And so the host mentioned above might have some reason for his dire prediction. The home and the Pentagon are struggling for the control of the minds of children.

Dan West, *Peace Education in Homes*, undated, Brethren Service Commission of the Church of the Brethren.

This makes the task of peace education much harder. And we may well ask whether the principles of following Jesus in the complex interdependent world—whether they can get into the minds of the next generation. I hold that they can—if parents are determined, resourceful, and intelligent about the whole matter. Then the question of HOW becomes a major one.

> The surviving documents demonstrate historically that the thing which we long called 'the moral consciousness of mankind' has grown up with each generation out of the discipline and the emotions of family life, supplemented by reflection and the teaching of experienced elders. The supreme values which lie within the human soul have therefore . . . entered the world for the first time through the operation of those gentle and ennobling influences which touch us continually in our family life. Whether in the beginning they were anywhere else out yonder in this vast universe, we shall never know; but they were not anywhere here upon our globe until the life of father, mother, and children created them. It was the sunshine and the atmosphere of our earliest human homes that created the ideals of conduct and revealed the beauty of self-forgetfulness.
>
> . . . There is one supreme human relationship, that which has created the home and made the family fireside the source out of which man's highest qualities have grown up to transform the world. As historical fact, it is to family life that we owe the greatest debt which the mind of man can conceive. The echoes of our own past from immemorial ages bid us unmistakably to venerate, to cherish, and to preserve a relationship to which the life of man owes this supreme debt.

> —James H. Breasted, *The Dawn of Conscience*

Now if Mr. Breasted is correct here, the essentials for peace education are the same as for good home life. In both cases it is a complex matter and calls for a fairly consistent way of living. Sometimes people who are very peaceful in their home life tend to be warlike in international matters. And maybe some who work hard for peace between nations lack something when it comes to home life. The job is never easy; and it is much harder to do than to plan. But I believe it can be done. I was that guest.

The whole pattern of requirements is somewhat more than what is given here, but these things seem to be essential:

A Good Diet

Children need an appropriate diet. So do the rest of the members of the family. Too little food prevents a healthy outlook. At the University of Minnesota some years ago a controlled experiment in starvation was run with some volunteer young men. I watched them eat—only a limited amount (they took in 1,800 calories a day and gave out 3,300 calories). One of them remarked, "How thin is the veneer of civilization when one is hungry."

This problem is the world's problem too. Not too much chance for peace on earth when so many are hungry all the time. Gandhi observed some years ago, "To a hungry man God is food."

But the kinds of food seem to make a difference also, in disposition and even in intelligence. "Tell me what you eat and I will tell you what you are." And there is deep meaning in the prayer: "Give us this day our daily bread" [Matt. 6:11].

Security

Children need a *sense of security*; so do parents. This means a friendly atmosphere. Children are especially sensitive; in a warm home they grow heartily. But in a hostile "home" they are worse off than a man without a country. Security, especially spiritual security, protects from some fears and antidotes others that do come in from the outside. Children need accurate information in response to their honest questions, spurs to courageous action, and steady examples of confidence and goodwill. "Perfect love casteth out fear" [1 John 4:18, KJV].

But security includes also a feeling of justice. When a child (or parent) does wrong, someone else must stand for the right; otherwise the foundations are shaken.

Further, security means many second chances—forgiveness. This does not annihilate the past, but it furnishes an antidote for wrong starts. The repentant "bankrupt" always needs new "credit."

> Happy is the family
> That has a true home
> Built by loyal hearts;
> For home is not a dwelling,
> But a living relationship.

And happy is the home
That is lighted by the torch of love,
For love is a flame
That cannot be blown out.

Wide Interests

Children need a *big* world—so do parents. "A wide range of interests is both a sign and a guard of sanity." The uncertainties of modern life tend to shrink the interests and to warp the imagination of many sensitive people. Shifting the attention often from suffering and hardship and "impossible" world problems to flowers, trees, and crops, to birds and pets, and to clouds and stars can help to restore perspective. Especially a wide knowledge of good people will help to make life not merely tolerable but triumphant. When a boy I was much impressed by the remark of a quiet visitor in our home. As I listened in wonder to his travels, he said, "I have always found good people everywhere I have gone."

A Major Cause

Children need a central interest or *cause* to organize these many interests—and so do parents. Otherwise "we want many things a little—nothing much." The Russians have a cause, and so have the Jews, the Negroes, the Asians, and many other groups. So had the Nazis, the American revolutionists, the early immigrants, the founders of the historic peace churches—and of every other church. We need the same cause which the early Christians had—and as much as they did.

More personal than a cause (maybe the inner core of a cause) is a *sense of destiny*, giving direction and drive to the life. Several examples: Mrs. Martin Niemöller is said to have asked their three sons about their future vocations when all of the family was suffering over the imprisonment of the father. As a minister he had opposed the Nazi plan. All three boys said they were going to become ministers.

In 1918 Ned Richards dared to test out the teaching against violence in Western Persia when his home was entered by Kurdish soldiers. In 1940 one of his sons refused to register because he could not become a part of a warring system. In his trial he said he wanted to carry on the record of his father.

In ancient times Moses chose rather to suffer affliction with the people of God than to enjoy the pleasures of sin for a season.

The Negro spirituals sometimes carried a sense of destiny. Here is one example: "I Know de Lawd Has Laid His Hands on Me."

Finding eternal values orients people from the future as well as from the past. The heritage of the historic peace churches, and others, can be used to develop adventurous spirits in a great cause.

Prayer

We do not know nearly enough about prayer; but even so, "more things are wrought by prayer than this world dreams of" [Alfred, Lord Tennyson]. As Richard Cabot wrote long ago: "Your soul and mine are parts of God. We forget this. Prayer reminds us."

Little children need a heavenly Father as well as one they can live with in a home. Prayer is a natural expression of "the soul's sincere desire." If from little up children are helped to pray they can stand better against the pressures of a military culture without weakening. And whatever our age we need to keep in steady connection with the spiritual world—"so strong to fight against all that is false and low and mean in life."

CREATING THE BACKGROUND

If we make a serious attempt to work on these essentials we need a setting or background. Otherwise results will not be at all what we desire. This is really an engineering task—but a good one. How can we start work on these elements? Here are some suggestions:

1. Set the examples you want your children to follow. Otherwise "what you are speaks so loud that I cannot hear what you say." Many deep beliefs and disciplines, both personal and group, are fixed before children are five years old. Interesting, too, that we parents are more likely to work harder on this matter if we do it for the sake of our children. Therefore no hurry—no worry.

2. Make your home the most friendly place your children can find. As fast as the children become able to help carry responsibility the "boss" idea should decrease—limit zero. And it is surprising how early this happens when children are loved; that is, by being sensitive to how they feel, by trying to understand them, and by trusting them.

3. Make home chores habitual by making them satisfactory. Chores are a good place to develop responsibility, but the *feelings* about the chores are of highest importance for educational purposes.

4. Help your children to big-muscle activities out of doors—both work and play. This eases off strain better than only small-muscle activities indoors—chiefly talking, looking, listening. We are built for action for the whole personality. It is good to build up activities about the need for food, clothing, and shelter.

5. Stress cooperative play—a hard job in a highly competitive society, such as ours. It is likely that our system of competitive sports does not make for peacemindedness; there is too much of the desire to win over some other person or group. Cooperative players in an orchestra make better music than competitive players. Once children learn that even in play the "power-with" activities are more fun than "power-over" activities they are set for "power-with" habits where they "play for keeps."

   Accepting the fact that play is a child's vocation, we still need to have a longer look if we are to develop the peace-minded children we want. It is as really true for us as for the Palestinian experiment of transplanted Jews to their old homeland that "even a good time must be endowed with some 'higher earnestness'; it must have some significant relationship to the general purpose of living."

6. Teach habits of relaxation, and make naps habitual for little children. Strain and fatigue are likely as damaging for peacemakers as for soldiers. Sitting together in loving silence can be helpful to every member of the family group.

7. In a world of hungry children teach your children to discipline their own desires for mere flavors after they have been well-fed. For example, after a good meal, can I eat whipped cream while some child lacks even skimmed milk? "Special privilege is the essence of immorality."

8. Cultivate a sense of humor. Children love it. And if it is real humor, there is no bitterness in it. Smiling eases strains. But teasing makes them worse.

9. Provide frequent chances for your children to make friends with children of other determined peacemakers. Here the new "primary" groups

are formed, and those groups make many of the decisions we "make." If the primary group to which your child belongs is headed for war, he will likely go too, or else break away at heavy cost to him, at least.

We need to do for the home what C. H. Cooley wrote in a school setting: "It is not to be supposed that the unity of the primary group is one of mere harmony and love. It is always a differentiated and usually competitive unity, admitting of self-assertion and various appropriative passions; but these passions are socialized by sympathy, and come . . . under the discipline of a common spirit. The individual will be ambitious, but the chief object of his ambition will be some desired place in the thoughts of others, and he will feel allegiance to common standards of service and fair play. So the boy will dispute with his fellows a place on the team, but above such disputes will place the common glory of class and school."

10. Invite the underprivileged in for meals, and especially invite adventurous spirits. This is better than asking too many of the "Joneses," or too often.

11. Make up for the hard blows received at school and elsewhere, but guard against pity; that is a weakening kind of factor in a child's life. Instead of that, talk over unpleasant events to "get all the terror out of them." Get your children used to "taking it."

On the positive side, touch the sense of the heroic in your children. Tom Sawyer had a poor system of ethics for our purposes, but he had the right idea when he wanted to get the other boys to whitewash the fence for him. He made the job seem both glamorous and hard.

William James half a century ago caught the idea we need here. "It is doubtful, indeed, whether a peaceful way of living will be achieved for modern men in terms of the traditional hymn-writer's conception of peace as a region of lilies and asphodels in the green pastures beside a murmuring brook. The old, the sick, the tired can be charmed by such visions; the young, the tough, and the resolute cannot. They *will* have their danger; they will have their struggle against obstacles."

J. Robert Oppenheimer spoke thus at the 200th anniversary of Columbia University: "This cannot be an easy life. We shall have a rugged time of it to keep our minds open and to keep them deep, to keep our sense of beauty and our ability to see it, in places remote and strange and unfamiliar. We shall have a rugged time of it, all of us, in keeping these gardens in our villages, in keeping open these manifold, intricate casual paths, to keep these flourishing in a great, open windy world. But this is, as I see it, the condition of man; and in this condition we can help it because we love one another."

Paul wrote some good advice to Timothy: "Take your share of suffering as a good soldier of Christ Jesus" [2 Tim. 2:3, NET].

12. Pull the family together and lift up the meanings of fun and strain and forgiveness and beauty into worship. This will be much different from "regular church services." The test: does it build lives on always higher levels?

13. Work to make your local church another "primary group," a friendly society which helps to make up for the lacks in other homes and other community agencies. This is too big a job for one home by itself.

14. Work for fellowship and cooperation with other churches and every other agency in the community that is "going our way." No use in assuming that *every* agency is headed in the direction of peace, but our invitation ought to be clear and steady.

15. Help to develop *a new culture* based on loving our neighbors as ourselves—in modern terms, respect for personality. Peace-mindedness will be one natural expression of that culture.

WORKING DIRECTLY

From the Negative Angle

We cannot ignore the negative side of peace education; and much of the direct work must oppose pressures toward war. Our ineffectiveness often shows up after we think we have done enough to insure steadiness enough. Here are some suggestions on several practical problems:

1. Don't talk much about war or war things. Talk rather about positive matters and good things to do, emphasizing those not yet done. "What gets your attention gets you."

2. Turn the radio and TV away from war news. "Whatsoever things are true ... honest ... just ... pure ... lovely ... of good report ... think on these

things" [Phil. 4:8, KJV]. The same will hold for newspapers. Maybe we should stop taking newspapers that promote war.

3. Avoid Bible stories about war for younger children. Later they can interpret them better.

4. Teach the children to hate—not people, but destructive attitudes, customs, and brutalizing forces, diseases and injurious insects, harmful bacteria, atom bombs, tanks, battleships, etc.

5. Where it is not possible to prevent war ideas and suggestions from coming to your children, shift their attention from instruments of war to the intended effects of those instruments, the destruction and suffering. Let them see the spiritual harm to those who use such instruments.

6. Furnish an antidote for personal ambition. Pronouns are really important. Teach the meanings of *we, ours,* and *us,* more than of *I, mine,* and *me* or *you* and *yours.*

7. Avoid serious comparisons of children's abilities and characteristics.

8. Minimize grade marks in school. There are better motives for learning and for satisfaction.

From the Positive Angle

Good living cannot be limited to negative things. There must be many vivid, glamorous *dos,* as well as some *don'ts.* The purpose here is to build new images in the mind—images of the peoples of the world needing one another, helping one another, acting toward one another with generous goodwill. Those images are better built early. The following are intended to help build that kind of image:

1. Read aloud and/or tell reliable stories of the heroes of peace. Save money elsewhere to provide materials for this. Help the children take part of this responsibility too.

2. Help them to talk out their trouble with each other—in the smallest group possible—to get it settled, to aim at making things right instead of proving who was right or wrong, to forgive quickly, to expect the other person to do better next time, to aim at the kind of justice which is guaranteed by love. This is an active—not a doormat—philosophy.

3. Teach the habits of self-reliance and cooperation *both*. "Every man shall bear his own burden" [Gal. 6:5, KJV]. "Bear ye one another's burden" [Gal. 6:2, KJV].

4. Point out the best values in your neighborhood. If you can honestly do it, try to make your children proud of your community.

5. Help the children to get acquainted with all the neighbors—those not quite respectable too. Beginning with the poor, build up the idea of loving all kinds of people—well dressed or poorly dressed, literate and illiterate, honest men and thieves. This calls for careful discrimination. But one small boy who hated war made the distinction. Speaking of a soldier visitor in the home, he said, "We can like him, even if we don't like his uniform."

    Build up the desire for travel and for doing it helpfully. Stress the best values of people who have different colors, different customs, different religions.

6. Teach that all people are the children of God, and that he is our Father.

7. Explain life, death, and danger in terms of cause and effect, but make clear that we understand only part of them. Teach your children to accept the universe with all its suffering, and then to rise above all the misery.

8. Stretch your children's imaginations toward the kind of world we ought to have, and put them to work to this end.

9. When your children have developed a firm trust in people, make them wise to propaganda and eager for the truth, both pleasant and unpleasant. "The truth shall make you free" [John 8:32, KJV].

10. Teach them to prize both organized government and organized religion, but to accept the domination of neither the church nor the state. Stress the value of the church now.

11. Teach the songs of peace, not the songs of war.

12. Teach loyalty to a world flag, more than to any national flag.

13. After the meanings are fairly clear, teach the scriptures that tell of the peace way of living, but not before the children understand them.

14. Find or make opportunities for your children to do something about their developing peace interests and convictions: projects that meet their readiness to do rather than only feel or think or talk.

METHODS OF EDUCATION

Getting the Attention

Until that happens education has not started. The best attention-getters are related to the main early interests of people: after food, they are women, children, and animals, according to one advertising psychologist. The most effective methods are:

1. Actual experience. "I was there" is convincing argument for education. Projects such as shoes, seeds, soap, and heifers have caught the attention of many people at different age levels.

2. Conversation in the home. What parents talk about is a powerful influence on children.

3. The art approaches.

    a. Pictures on the wall, in papers, books, slides, filmstrips, or moving pictures. "Third dimension" pictures, if in color, look much like the real thing. "One picture is worth a thousand words." The home job is selection mainly. Pictures to draw or color may be helpful too.

    b. Stories, "the living word," are the basis for real tradition. [N. F. S.] Grundtvig proved this again with his Danes nearly a century ago. Phonograph records have high value even if the message is "canned." Radio stories and plays are powerful methods. Television has untold possibilities.

    c. Music. "Let me write the songs of a nation: I don't care who writes the laws."

    d. Symbols. Flags have high teaching value. A world flag might well be in every home. Souvenirs and museum pieces carry meanings, too.

4. Written word approaches. Leaflets, pamphlets, and books—the most abused methods, but helpful when used wisely.

    "Whatever gets your attention gets you."

Guiding the Attention

Holding and guiding the attention is a tougher job than getting it. The old army pattern of command and obedience and drill, drill, drill will not well fit our purposes. But we need drill of a kind.

The right to do this cannot be assumed—it has to be earned. If our children really trust us even after all the mistakes we keep on making and with all of our customary rigidity of thinking, they will tend to take on the highest values we ourselves hold. And they may go beyond that.

But there are difficult and important possibilities in learning about the problems of the modern world. Since children will have to live in this kind of world, we owe it to them to help understand it. This takes hard "skull work." Here most parents are lazy—leave it to the teacher, Sunday school teacher, or somebody else. It shows up as a bad thing in many places.

A Catholic friend of mine likes to remind me: "You Protestant parents don't take on the responsibility that belongs to you. You turn over the education of your children to other people. Of course you have to have help—but it is your job."

[Auguste] Buisseret, the Belgian Minister of Education, reported that the Nazis had done some very effective work on Belgian children during the occupation period. After 45-minute lectures, 10-minute films were shown; then an examination was given on each topic "to impress the theme still more firmly on their minds." They had "8,000 lantern-slides, all attractively designed to capture the imagination and stimulate the loyalty of the youngsters to Hitler's ideology and practices."

"Also, they had reproductions of Aztec vases, spearheads, and other articles of Indian origin, each of which carried among its hieroglyphs the swastika. This set was designed to create in the childish minds both veneration for the antiquity and admiration for the artistry of the Nazi Party symbol."

For our purpose 45-minute lectures are too long. Films could be borrowed from churches for home use. Discussion would be much better than an examination. Books and pamphlets of the right kind can be of great help in guiding the attention.

Heroes—Prodigals—or What?

As the war develops an increasing number of people come to accept it as the right thing, and to believe that those who take part in war are doing the right thing. It creeps.

Someday the boys will come back home. Those who have been injured in body and mind are already coming back home by the thousands. That number will increase. When the able-bodied come back, church folks and others will have something of a problem as to how to receive them. We might think of them all as heroes. It is traditional to do that. And because they have had priorities on many things, some of them may come to expect it to continue. They may come to believe that they really are heroes. If so, it is quite possible that the military tradition which we deplore so much in Germany and other countries will become part of our American tradition, and even of Christian tradition. That tradition produces more wars. "So long as we deck the brow of a soldier with laurels, so long we shall have wars."

On the other hand, as more people become disgusted with the business of killing their fellow men, there is a possibility of reaction in another direction. I have not a doubt that many of the soldiers will repent bitterly for their part in the destruction of life and property. They may come to look down on themselves and we may be in some danger of looking down on them. Some of us who have not taken active part in the war may develop the attitude of the older brother of the prodigal son, and be hard-hearted toward our men now in the armed forces. That attitude would certainly destroy the spirit of brotherhood.

There is a third possibility. We have not yet done a thorough job of teaching our peace doctrine to our own youth. In some cases they have never heard of it. In others, "peace teaching" had no genuine enthusiasm back of it; and so it never touched their imaginations. In still other cases we were reluctant about furnishing the economic support for the dependents of those who wanted to stand for the thing our church has taught. Again, we have sometimes called ourselves pacifists because we objected to the effects of war;

Dan West, "Heroes—Prodigals—or What?," undated, box 49, Dan West Papers, Brethren Historical Library and Archives.

at the same time we have been very enthusiastic and warm toward economic advantages, feelings of racial superiority, and nationalistic development. We have not always recognized that these things are the natural causes of war.

Maybe it would be right for all of us to be more humble. At our best we are still unprofitable servants. Certainly it would be right for those of us at home to repent for whatever attitudes, whatever advantages, whatever words have been ours which do not fit with our peace doctrine. Maybe we're all prodigals in some sense. If we are humble and honest, if we are determined that the faith of our fathers is going on to our sons in spite of war and in spite of our own weaknesses, we shall be in better position to welcome our boys, to bind up the wounds of the spirit, and to work with both the men from the armed forces and from CPS [Civilian Public Service] camps toward building a finer church than we've ever had. If we start on that, we can build finer communities than we have ever had. That will make possible our biggest contribution to the age-old dream of "peace on earth, goodwill to men."

According to Bernard Iddings Bell in a recent article in *Harper's Magazine*, we are unwise to expect the war to transform men into something better than the churches were able to develop before the war: If they drank liquor before, if they were loose on sex matters, or if they were irreverent, they will likely become more so because of the war; on the other hand, if the drafted men really loved God at heart these values are likely to be intensified by the war. Some people now as during the first world war are very hopeful of the idealism of most of us after the war is over, but a thoughtful writer spoke in 1919, "Human nature is capable of infinite heroism upon occasion. It slumps badly when the occasion passes."

I see no way to avoid a letdown after the war except among those with deep spiritual roots; and the sifting of the afterwar conditions will test us all thoroughly. But I propose that we get ready for that testing, somewhat thus:

1. Let us recognize the heroic spirit everywhere we find it. A Marine shot down while carrying a wounded comrade back to "safety"; a CPS man swept out to sea while hunting for the body of a Navy airman; another CPS man electrocuted while trying (in the absence of an expert) to bring light and power back to a hospital; the patient, steady work of a mother who carries on at home under suffering—and in hundreds of other places.

2. Let us recognize that we have all "sinned, and come short of the glory of God" [Romans 3:23, KJV]—all of us, including the most ardent pacifists, the busiest workers and writers, the most patient teachers, the most ardent speakers, the ace who has brought down a high quota of "enemy" planes, the farmer or war worker who has made and kept blood money—and let us repent for having done so little to build the kind of world which will eliminate war. As one young mother wrote about her soldier brother who was killed last winter, "I don't blame him, I only blame myself and the other more mature members of my family and the local church that we didn't do more to influence his thinking when he was younger."

3. Let us not get too much enjoyment out of either heroic living or repentance. As one thoughtful observer put it, "A certain man boiled with rage at his own idleness—but he was content to idly boil." Let us begin now to reach out our sympathies to all the flounderers better than the old hen who spreads her wings to gather in all the chickens. Let us reorganize our attitudes and other habit patterns on economic matters, on matters of forgiveness, matters of race, and especially on our typical religion of nationalism even while we claim to be following the Master. We may all be heroes in some points, cowards in others; but whatever we are we can become exemplars in the way of the Master.

VII.

MISSION TO THE WORLD

⌒⌒⌒

I am," **Dan West wrote,** "a sober optimist." In his 1966 moderator's address, West praised Church of the Brethren programs including missions, workcamps, and Heifer Project, local congregations, and even denominational staff, but remained suspicious of the increasingly suburban orientation of American church and society in the postwar years. West felt the church must heed Paul Tillich's warning: "If the church ever dies in America, it will die in suburbia from its own respectability."

In the second document, West, in the spirit of other social gospel-oriented progressives, urged the creation of a culture of interdependency, not independence.

In the final document, published in celebration of the two-hundred-fiftieth anniversary of the Church of the Brethren, West dealt with the perennial Brethren and Christian issue of the church–state relations. Unlike many young Brethren radicals, West maintained a generally positive view of the promise of America. "The state," West wrote, "is a wonderful servant, but a very hard master." Rejecting the anarchy he had witnessed during the Spanish Civil War, sectarian withdrawal from society, and unconditional obedience to the state, West urged personal and group discipline to help transform the state toward one of Christian brotherhood. The unfinished social mission of the church was to move "the kingdom of the world" into "the kingdom of our Lord and of his Christ."

⌒⌒⌒

Not to Destroy but to Fulfill

Annual Conference is our big family reunion, and I am glad we are here. Fellowship has been one of the specialties of Brethren and must continue if the church is to endure. Mutual love is a valid badge of discipleship, Jesus said. But there are purposes beyond this: hard problems to be solved. Problems too big to be handled locally are being dished up increasingly by our rapidly changing world. Some Brethren are gloomy, but I am a sober optimist.

We Are Each an Important Person

There is a danger that some may feel more important than others. An able organist was giving a concert one night years ago. Things went well. The audience was responsive and enthusiastic. At the intermission, the boy who had been pumping the organ was excited too. He came down off his platform and said to the organist, "That was a good job we did!" The organist replied solemnly, "That was a good job *I* did." The boy was silent as he climbed back to his place. Soon the organist took his seat and motioned for the pumping to begin again. But nothing happened. This annoyed him and the audience was waiting. He motioned again and commanded in a whisper, "Start *pumping*." The boy looked him straight in the eye and spoke back, "Say 'we' first."

All of us are important here. I am glad we have both conservatives and liberals here. We need all of you if you are really trying to be honest and are steadily seeking the mind of Christ. Every one of us knows something about the church that others of us do not. We need to build solidly a genuine base of Christian brotherhood both for ourselves and for the greater world that God also loves.

We Live in a Perilous World

There are many forces which are playing hard on our lives, our homes, our churches, and the larger world we live in. One of these is increasing change. The changing church is much more influenced by the changing world than ever before. No wonder. The world is crowding in on us harder than ever. There is no hiding place. The farm home is not what it used to be. The racial problem in the United States and South Africa and the war in Vietnam are

---

Dan West, "Not to Destroy but to Fulfill," *Messenger*, July 7, 1966.

just two of the insistent problems. But others may loom before 1970; possibly World War III, a depression, a degenerating Western culture, and certainly hunger on a bigger scale. We are not yet ready to meet these or other problems. But we must get ready.

Another force is increasing awareness. The church is becoming aware that many other people are concerned too—both Christians and non-Christians. I will guess that nobody here tonight believes that Brethren have a corner on God. We need the help of everyone who will work with us if we are to have peace on earth. How to relate to other Christians and other people is a real problem. We shall deal with part of that at this Conference.

A third force is confusion. The church is more confused than I have ever seen it before. Some Brethren seem to believe that everything is changing. Many youth are like sheep without a shepherd. A very able old-time church worker described a recent type of leader as "an enlightened religious scholar who verbalizes freely, feels a superior degree of understanding, but is afraid to state all he understands. His beliefs are vague. His basic thinking becomes both cyclical and blurred as he approaches life's great issues." None of the rest of us has the answers either. And as lazy and sometimes cruel as we laymen have been, I can see why some good pastors become discouraged. Unless more of us become more honest and responsible with more nerve to act out what we claim to believe, the church is headed for greater confusion.

We Have Abundant Resources

One of our resources is our Brethren culture. If anyone present wants to ignore the past and deal only with the here and now, I want to speak to you here and now. Maybe you hate down deep the culture which produced you. Because that was once true of me, I can understand. For a long time it was mainly subconscious. If I can help you, I want to. Here is a start: It could not have been *all* bad, since it produced you. I have no doubt about your finding valuable assets in your home, as well as some liabilities. No, I am not favoring ancestor worship, just honest bookkeeping. If we fulfill the best from our home culture, we can look our children in the eye and urge them to do better than we. Then they can urge their children to improve on that. From now on there will be plenty of room for improvement. Hard work? Certainly.

Another resource much more ancient than our church is the Bible. Many have tried to use this resource fully, even though most of us are very ignorant of it. It has been compared to a signpost for travelers. But we Christians have spent more time worshiping the signpost than following the road. For me the New Testament is a gambler's handbook giving rules for betting our lives that Jesus is the way, the truth, and the life in our changing and confusing world.

A third resource is our record as a church. Honest bookkeeping here is also appropriate:

Our mission work. Begun in the nineteenth century, it has been a good thing for the kingdom. I never became excited about missions until I saw our work in several Indian villages.

Workcamps. They were started in the United States in 1934 by the Quakers; we worked with them a little and have done something on our own. A real risk now: Some people think they are condescending.

Conscientious objectors. The trees planted in the early 1940s are very beautiful now—those that survived.

Heifer Project. The Brethren began it, but twenty years ago we did more for it than now.

Cooperation with other churches. This includes such organizations as Church World Service, CROP, Agricultural Missions, Fraternal Relations. Of course, there are frustrations.

Brethren Volunteer Service. This was sparked by the youth themselves. There have been some casualties, but the net value has been high. Here is a great resource for the changing world.

The people in our church right now, especially the laymen, are a resource. [Toyohiko] Kagawa once said, "In America you have the finest biological stock in the world." That sounds pleasant to some of us here whether it is true or not. Anyhow, some of it is in the Church of the Brethren.

If we had conserved without any force in religion our own youth the little Church of the Brethren would be much larger than it is. It is good that some did stay by. I am convinced that the present shrinkage could be stopped. In a number of places from Pennsylvania to California I have asked groups of youth the same question, "Do you feel that the older folks in your church really care for you?" In only one place, a small church in Michigan, was there a unanimous yes. But in every other place there was a plurality of favorable responses. One girl in a group of about twenty-five added, "Yes, they care, but they don't know how to show it."

Then there are our churches. For many years the urban forces have pulled too many of our ablest people away. But some are still in rural areas. And the large majority of our churches are in rural areas. In the past fifteen to twenty years we may have bargained for some white elephants in suburbia. Well, let us finish paying for them if we can harness them up to the world's problems, heeding the warning of Paul Tillich some years ago, "If the church ever dies in America, it will die in suburbia from its own respectability."

Organizations are part of our resources. For many years I have been critical of a number of things in the Church of the Brethren including our organizations and their functioning. And I still am. But also I am increasingly grateful for some new developments which I have had a good chance to know firsthand. In the thirty-eight years since I began to work with "Elgin" my respect for the General Brotherhood Board is higher now than ever before. If you have studied their report you will notice a new honesty about our situation—even when it hurts. Also, I have watched a growth in brotherhood and responsibility in its work. Here is a great resource. I believe the General Brotherhood Board is moving in the right direction mainly and so is worthy of your greater confidence and our best constructive criticism.

We Can Minister in the World

I am offering some concrete recommendations here, maybe for the Conference, but certainly for local churches and districts and possibly for future Conferences before 1970.

1. Select a few major problems in addition to the prescribed duties we have to care for. We cannot hope to digest all the smorgasbord of problems, but can deal with a few basics such as the home and peace on earth.

2. Look at all the possible ways for us to solve these problems. One university professor of mine regrets that "we suffer from a poverty of alternatives." We must become increasingly intelligent in our planning.

3. Select the best from Brethren and other heritages (the measure is always the mind of Christ) and bid steadily for the hearty cooperation of all other groups "going our way." This would increase our resources and make a clearer witness. If that should lead to merger with one or more churches someday, we could thank God.

4. Get into action as fast as we can plan and then mobilize our resources to witness that Jesus is "the way, the truth, and the life" for us in the rapidly

changing world. This would certainly mean stress and sacrifice, maybe even ridicule or stronger opposition. But Jesus never promised anybody an easy life.

If we prove to our youth that we really care for them and then catch their imaginations for heroic service that fits with the mind of Christ, we could improve the quality of and then double our present missionary programs, including Brethren Volunteer Service. Further, if we can convince qualified middle-aged parents without heavy family responsibilities that they may serve well away from home even without extensive schooling, they could be sent on missions with the literacy or Peace Corps or other constructive programs. The rest of us at home could support them without any real hardship. Two cents a day for a year from only one half of our membership could support one hundred and fifty more of them. And God's world might be served better.

If we want to save children's lives from starvation, we could easily send one heifer or the equivalent with another source of animal protein per church every year. One cent a day extra from only one half of our members would do it. And when responsible receivers of our living gift of 1,130 heifers "passes on the gift" to other needy families, thousands of lives could be saved.

Do We Care?

Unless we do far better on leadership training than we have ever done, we shall not be able to give any better witness before 1970 or afterward. Enough experiments have happened in the past ten years to warrant a much bigger program than we ever had. Mission Twelve has been another good beginning. And new discoveries are happening all the time. If we put this first on our internal plans for the church by 1970 we might have the leadership we ought to have right now. And that might be better for the human race than putting a man on the moon by 1970.

Still a Sober Optimist

I believe that the little Church of the Brethren has "come to the kingdom for such a time as this" [Esther 4:14, KJV]. If we are determined to seek first his kingdom and his righteousness we shall never destroy the best that has come down to us but will help to fulfill the scripture, "Greater things than these shall ye do . . ." [John 14:12, KJV adapted]. The time may be very short. What this Conference decides may one day have an enormous effect on the world that God loves.

Still Proclaiming

With the growth of deep Christian faith comes a new self-respect; it is not possible to hold in slavery people who believe themselves to be sons of God. Also with this faith comes a new sensitivity to the welfare of other people. From these roots come new dreams.

Nearly two centuries ago—1752—someone dreamed of liberty for the colonists of the "new world." And the Assembly of the province of Pennsylvania ordered the making of a bell with these words near the rim: "Proclaim liberty throughout all the land unto all the inhabitants thereof" [Lev. 25:10, KJV].

Twenty-four years later—1776—the same bell became the Liberty Bell. Freedom, liberty, independence—these words have become almost commonplace, except for those whose skins are too dark or whose jobs depend on world markets and some other people. Not all the inhabitants have heard the real message of liberty yet. But freedom for those who have heard does not stay put; it has come and gone in many places. And not yet have we Americans learned all of the responsibility that goes with freedom.

Now there is a new world in a new sense. Will freedom survive, or will there be a struggle for power that will end in the peace of the cemetery? Some people have lost faith in freedom, but others are just as hopeful and as determined as were our American forefathers. In India they seem to have learned new ways to secure freedom.

More than forty years ago Theodore Roosevelt pled for a Declaration of Interdependence. Maybe he was right.

It is time for a new growth of Christian faith. Could we pick up the essential meanings of the early American dream, and the meanings of the earlier Hebrew dream, and proclaim a message like this: "Proclaim liberty of body and mind and spirit through all the world unto all the inhabitants thereof."

Dan West, July 1949, box 50, Dan West Papers, Brethren Historical Library and Archives.

The Brethren and the Modern State

The Annual Conference of 1908, celebrating the bicentennial of the Church of the Brethren, began with thinking about the problem of government. The first address then had to do with church polity or government *within* the church. It may be more than a coincidence that the program committee set a similar problem as the beginning of our thought for this Annual Conference celebrating the two-hundred-fiftieth anniversary of the founding of the church. But this time the thought is to be government *outside* the church—the relation of the Brethren to the modern state.

Brethren always live under tension. The more we try to live our doctrines in the modern world, the more the tensions increase and the heavier they become. One of the greatest tensions for Christians everywhere comes out of the relation between church and state. And one of the heaviest for the Church of the Brethren comes in relation to the American nation-state. We Brethren always love our country, respect many of its customs, and obey its laws. But we have some doubts about the actual state. (For present thinking, the word *state* refers chiefly to government officials—persons who are authorized to act for the state.)

Government Is Right

We Brethren believe in government as a matter of principle. We have scripture for it: "The powers that be are ordained of God" (Romans 13:1*b*, KJV). And Brethren have always accepted the governments they find—sometimes too well. We have never been political revolutionaries.

For some people on this planet, however, government is a bad thing and anarchy is their goal. In the family it may be only a temporary affair when youth try to develop independence from their elders and become persons in their own right. They seem to be anarchistic but they do accept a great deal of tyranny from their peers. Most of them, however, go on later to learn interdependence. That means some kind of government.

However, there have been sizable groups of even adults who claim not to believe in any organized government at all. During the Spanish Civil War,

---

Dan West, "The Brethren and the Modern State," in *The Adventurous Future*, ed. Paul H. Bowman (Elgin, IL: Brethren Press, 1959), 117-31.

on many telephone poles in Barcelona posters appeared bearing [Mikhail] Bakunin's picture and this message in Spanish: "Anarchy is the highest form of order."

Brethren would not agree to this. Anarchy is not the highest form of order.

The Modern State

The state is a wonderful servant, but a very hard master. And the tendency is always toward too much control and too little real responsibility. Today the state as we know it exerts more control over its people than Brethren can welcome. Now some controls are necessary, but for the best human welfare there must be a limit. We accept some controls, such as traffic laws, taxes, and wage controls, cheerfully—or soberly. Other controls, such as draft laws and some civil defense items, we accept with reservation. But when the state goes too far, the Brethren say no and mean it. For example, in a small town near the Canadian border, one civil defense official from the state headquarters was explaining that a warden had been appointed over every designated area in the town. "And that man's word is law," he said bluntly.

Quickly there came a response. Two ministers (one a Dunkard) objected, saying, "That man's word is not law. This is America." Immediately the imposing-looking "house of cards" crumbled.

During most of the nineteenth century the state let us alone quite largely and we let it alone. However, in the modern world this is no longer possible either for us or for the state. Neither can let the other alone. And in the future, it seems, tensions from state controls will increase more yet.

One regional planner from Harvard University predicted that "rigid governmental and economic controls beyond all we have ever known will be required to place the community interest—and common good—before the so-called rights of individuals."

Another example: Luther Gulick of the New York City Institute of Public Administration believes that one fact is going to force us into a new type of thinking: "Most Americans will be born, grow up and live, work and die in great city areas." And he expects governmental structures to handle the problems that develop.

If these predictions are correct, every decade will bring Brethren and all other Christian groups (and everybody else) under more controls and into heavier tension with the state. But there are real dangers here. Let us look at a few of them.

1. **Some people tend to glorify the state.** The flag worship before important public events is one evidence of this. Flags in churches are worth studying also. Some people seem to imagine that the state has almost personal qualities and demands a supreme loyalty. In their minds, the state is no longer a servant; it is a master. One high school valedictorian this spring put the law of the land before the law of God. But this deification of the state is pure fiction. Professor [William Ernest] Hocking would remind Brethren and everybody else that "there is no state entity, but there is a God."

Now governments are not all alike. But too many similarities seem to develop with time in modern states as well as in ancient ones. Governments tend to go beyond the restraint of evildoers in the direction of restraining the activities of persons and groups toward justice and toward common welfare. State officials are not impersonal administrators of law, but often very faulty persons like the rest of us. Sometimes they don't even average up. Then, if they are power hungry, they will tend to reach farther and farther toward increasing control of the people.

So long as the state "is not a terror to good works," Brethren feel little tension. But if governments encroach on human rights or attempt to control the church, tension increases heavily. And this is happening in America and other modern states. More than ten years ago Lord [John] Boyd Orr, then director-general of the Food and Agriculture Organization of the United Nations, complained rather bitterly over the typical attitude of government officials at the United Nations assembly. Soon after his report and his plea for more help for the hungry people of the world, he shared some of his sadness with me: "It seems that governments are more concerned about political advantage than they are about the welfare of their own people." Half a century ago, [Lord John] Acton saw this process also and he reminded us that "power always tends to corrupt. Absolute power corrupts absolutely."

Some thinkers believe that all modern states will go totalitarian. One novelist attempted to describe the breaking of the last human personality in the process of making him into a willing tool of the state.

In summary, there are risks as well as gains in the development of states. Brethren should be aware of both of them. Any state worship combined with grasping for power over people is dangerous. Obedience to the state is better than anarchy, but it is not the highest form of order. Here, too, "eternal vigilance is the price of liberty," as much as in Thomas Jefferson's day.

2. **National sovereignty is overemphasized.** The modern state accepts too little responsibility for the welfare of people outside. Often they are ignored and most of the time they are treated as of less importance than people within any given state. As transportation and communication bring us closer together, this becomes a dangerous policy. The weather has never had any respect for national boundaries; nor have radio waves, influenza germs, hunger, or even ideas. More recently, earth satellites have no respect for national boundaries; neither has radioactive fallout.

We should be grateful for the heroic service to mankind by the United Nations but at the same time aware of its weaknesses. Here is one: The United Nations is still based on the idea of national sovereignty—every state doing as it pleases. This is just a more respectable name for international anarchy. The worship of the state feeds this dangerous idea. And the present obsession with war plans is both a result and a new case of anarchy between states. There is an increasing need for a world government, instead of international anarchy. Now, we are more than ever before "in the same boat."

To summarize:

- Brethren accept some state controls. Anarchy is not the highest form of order.
- We cannot worship any state, nor obey it blindly. Obedience to the state is not the highest form of order.
- Our faith is worldwide and reaches beyond the confines of national sovereignty.

We oppose the idea of anarchy either among persons or between states. National sovereignty is not the highest form of order. By the way, church sovereignty is not the highest form of order either. Anarchy is as wrong between Christian groups as between states or people.

This tension which comes from accepting government and yet having doubts about it makes a difficult problem for Brethren to work out. What are the best relationships to the modern state?

Possible Relationships to the State

With the prospect of present tensions increasing and newer and greater ones developing in the future, it may be helpful to look at all possible ways of meeting them. There are two main types—running away or staying by.

1. **We could run away.** This is the "avoidance reaction" of which the biologists tell us. It can be either a physical or a spiritual running away. This sometimes does solve one part of a problem anyhow.

A. *By emigrating.* Abraham did this; we do not know exactly for what reason. Moses and the Hebrew children left Egypt when tension with the state became too great. So did the Pilgrims, the Catholics, and the Quakers, from England. From Germany, the Mennonites and the Brethren. There have been many more groups. The national Hungarians are the most recent evidence of emigration as a way of meeting too much tension with the state. Not many years ago a small group of Quakers emigrated to Costa Rica apparently to get away from the problems connected with the military draft. As we look back on most of these efforts, we are inclined to commend the persons involved for taking this way out.

But in our modern world we have a tough problem. There is no longer any place to go with any assurance for any long time. Geographical migration does not seem to be a way out for us.

B. *By going into a monastery.* As we learn more of the history of the church we have an increasing reason to be grateful for the monastery, which helped to conserve the Christian faith during the Dark Ages. Professor Floyd Mallott was of the opinion that the denominations under great stress might serve in our time a function similar to that of the monasteries during the Dark Ages. The Bruderhof movement may be a monastic movement, although some of its apologists do not think so. Insofar as it is a withdrawal from the problems incurred from the relationship of the state, it may be monastic. If state persecution comes, this—as a last resort—might be justifiable. But until then, hardly for the Brethren. We are living *in* the world, partly because we have to. But more than that—we want to.

C. *By going into a "holy" vocation.* Here is a delicate problem. In the United States and in some other countries, clergymen have been exempt from military draft for a long time. And it is defended by some thinkers. It does give more freedom for them; but it does raise a doubt about what is God's will. Does he have one will for his special servants and a different will for the rest of us?

This holy-vocation method of running away has further implications, however. Alex Miller in his provocative book, *Christian Faith and My Job*, gives the opinion that the people who work in "uplift" jobs such as the ministry, social work, and teaching are really dodging the hard problems which the rest of us must face. If we Brethren are to find a real answer to this question, we ought to grapple with more of the problems the majority of mankind has to meet. From our former sheltered life, we may have become too naïve.

2. **We could stay by.** We are not inclined to run away—at least not many of us—but more and more it will become impossible for us Brethren to run away if we wanted to. And so, we must look at the other alternatives.

We ought to have a better reason—that of wanting to stay by in order to give the witness to our faith and to help in the carrying out of our responsibilities in some way. There are different ways of doing this also. Here are four of them:

A. *Accepting the demands of the state as the will of God—"adjusting."* A modern rationalization of this appears in a proverb: "If you can't fight 'em, join 'em." Most churches have done this as a matter of principle, but it is foreign to the Brethren belief. However, under stress some Brethren officials have made some major "adjustments." I mention one.

When World War I was declared in 1917, the Brethren were not ready for that kind of strain. In the uncertainty, a special Conference was called at Goshen, Indiana, in January 1918. There, after some discussion, a statement was drawn up for the guidance of the Brethren who might be affected by the war and the draft. It looks fairly harmless now, but when it came to the attention of the War Department it was considered seditious. Accordingly, some Brethren officials were called to meet some state officials. One of our men described it thus to me later: "We almost got down on our knees before Secretary [Newton] Baker to take back the Goshen statement."

The first thing for me to remember is that I was not there, and so I have no judgment to offer against the men who were there. However, I cannot stop thinking about it or wondering what John Kline would have done—or Christopher Sauer, or John Naas, or other Brethren leaders in former times. Certainly I cannot fit that with anything I read about the early church in a situation where the tensions might have been even heavier. Yes, to be honest about it, we must admit that the Brethren have "adjusted" on some occasions.

Now to take the brown taste out of the mouth, let us look at an incident where the Brethren did not "adjust." It was during World War II. For some reason some official in Washington decided that Civilian Public Service men (who were engaged in alternative service) were to be ordered to cut their way through the forest to a certain kind of timber thought best for airplane propellers. It was clearly for war purposes, and they were to do this under military guard if necessary. Well, another church official under that stress gave the instruction to collapse Civilian Public Service if necessary. This was a distinct *no* to the state.

To improve the taste a little more, another incident may be worth reporting. The Japanese were uprooted from the West Coast because of a supposed military danger. One fine Japanese boy in Civilian Public Service had been considered by church and state officials. And it was agreed that he would be left alone unless some unfavorable publicity should compel his transfer. But one state man changed his mind and ordered him to be shifted on very short notice. A church official presented this problem to the whole group of Civilian Public Service men at suppertime, and they united against the edict. Yes, there were plans to put the whole group into jail. But plans were worked out so that that was not necessary. (Some thought this action was an "adjustment.")

Brethren can sometimes say no to the state. And there may be more such occasions in the future, under the greater tensions, because we cannot have another master once we accept the lordship of Christ.

B. *Splitting the personality.* "My heart belongs to God, my body to the state." These are heavy words from an important source. But before we censure Martin Luther for them, we may well be very humble ourselves. We had better take a little time to study our own integrity—or lack of it—under stress. Maybe we, too, have separated part of our activities from our religion. Many of us working in defense plants or taking and keeping "blood money" from war sources (I mean the extra purchasing power) have allowed our own personalities to be split. But Brethren consciences are restless under all such incidents. This is not the best way to stay by.

C. *Transforming the state.* With our new and growing sense of responsibility for what happens in our country we are trying to help to move the state in the direction of a Christian policy. And it takes "the long look of faith" (as

W. W. Slabaugh put it); but it is commendable that an increasing number of Brethren are trying to help carry that burden.

However, this means more than just voting or telling Congressmen what we feel on important issues. It is as Professor John Brierly of Cambridge University gave it to a little handful in Geneva, Switzerland, thirty years ago: "It is your job to create the spiritual stuff out of which international law is made." This will mean long, hard toil—even agony. It includes minor compromises, with the steady temptation to make major compromises But we can hold steady under that tension, too. "Something is borne because something is being born."[1] Brethren can contribute something toward sound government within the state and beyond it toward a sound world government. This is staying by and doing something constructive.

Some people do not believe that the state will ever be transformed, and they can find much evidence for their position. But there are some others who see further. Some years ago Jan Smuts, the former field marshal and empire builder from South Africa, was talking with Andrew Cordier at the United Nations center in New York City. When [Hartley] Shawcross, the British delegate was mentioned, Smuts asked if he were not a Quaker. Cordier did not know. "I believe he is," the old warrior went on. "Anyhow, he has Quaker background. . . . You know, humanity is very tired of war. It has lost the way. The Quakers have that way. Sometime we shall have to come to that philosophy for the basis of our political decisions."

[Toyohiko] Kagawa is hopeful for his county. He said: "We are going to alter the definition of a great state. A truly great state is not necessarily big, nor rich, nor quarrelsome with its neighbor. The great state is wise, moral, and God-fearing. We aim to make Japan a state with which God can be pleased."

Brethren must help make America a state with which God can be pleased.

D. *Personal and group discipleship.* This means living in the modern state, but keeping spiritually clean. In this position Brethren will do what they can to carry the burdens of the state, but that is not their central task. They will not put all their eggs in that basket—nor most of them. Several comparisons might be helpful here, although they do not fit exactly. A lifeguard does all he can to teach others to swim and in an emergency to save someone from drowning. But he is not willing to drown also if he fails to save the victim. In a world of disease, doctors try to keep themselves healthy. In a real sense

---

1. Hocking, W. E., in *The Coming World Civilization.*

anyone taking this position is not *of* the world while he lives *in* the world. Brotherhood under the lordship of Christ means that whenever it comes to the choice between transforming the state and keeping the conscience unspotted from the world, "we must obey God rather than man." This is the major responsibility of Brethren in the modern state.

Toward the Right Relationship

1. **State and church should recognize that both are needed in a good society.** Each one can do something, but not everything. Hocking makes much of the state's impotence[2] to motivate or furnish standards for its own functions, to provide the basis for education or for punishment, to stabilize the family or the economy. It cannot even control its own moral sources in the field of recreation. He thinks that the more complex life becomes the more the state needs the church to furnish motivation and standards for the chief functions of society, including those of the state.

2. **The central motives of love and justice are valid for both church and state.** At its best the state may be interested in love, but it insists on justice. The church, at its best, seeks justice, but it insists on love. The church cannot shift that central motivation. The state can implement what love creates. As [Tomáš] Masaryk put it, "justice is the arithmetic of love."

Both of them are concerned about values which extend beyond any human life. The state has longer vision than any person. That of the church is infinitely longer—eternal. The state deals with the present world; the church does also, but it reaches beyond. Brethren need to prepare themselves for both worlds at the same time.

3. **"Power-with" the state.** Brethren cannot say that the church is self-sufficient without the state. For the best living we need the state, but we desire no blind acceptance of it. And we favor a continued separation of church and state.

The time was when the church had power over the state. And recently the state has gained almost complete control over the church in some countries. We cannot accept either condition. Our target is a genuine interdependence. Like the fungus and the alga which cooperate in the lowly lichen that grows on rocks and produces soil, like the bacteria which lives in the rumens in cattle and other cud-chewing animals, like the fig moth and the fig which help

---

2. Hocking, 7-15.

each other, so church and state will become increasingly interdependent in an increasingly complex world. Biologists call it symbiosis. Here, however, the church is the prime mover of the pair. The church furnishes the eggs and hatches them; the state rightly furnishes the laying house. Hocking says that "the state is dependent for its vital motivation upon an independent, religious community."[3] Brethren cannot be content with any kind of anarchy.

States must come to learn the "power-with" principle also—a larger symbiosis. If churches learn it first, they can be more convincing to states.

4. **The state is right in putting some tension on the church for basic motivation and for standards of the good life.** And, more than either of these, for examples of good living. *Fortune* magazine made an appeal of this type to churches at the beginning of World War II. Schools, hospitals, relief agencies, and many others have been born in the church and taken over by state officials. Many ideas on technical assistance came largely from the efforts of missionaries. This is right. The state can serve society by not allowing the church to become smug or lazy. Religious liberty is a wonderful blessing. But if we ever take it for granted, it will trickle through our fingers. The state can help the Brethren appreciate religious liberty by insisting that it be re-earned locally in every generation. If we have to go a thousand miles or a hundred years away for new evidence, it is never quite convincing to us or to the state—or to our youth.

5. **The church must also keep a tension on the state in the direction of:**

A. *Honesty.* "The whole art of government consists in the art of being honest," said Thomas Jefferson.

B. *Religious freedom as the complexities of life increase.* This includes freedom for everybody, not just for our little group. This toleration of minorities is often awkward. It means a "war of persuasion in a world of free wills."

C. *Human welfare on a world scale.* The church must also keep a tension on the state to enlarge horizons to take in more people and the larger welfare of the whole world. This has been happening, but it must increase. This includes: food for every person on a basis that builds self-respect; health for every person within the limits of knowledge; education for every person to both the privileges and the responsibilities of world citizenship; and learning to live together helpfully as people on a "shrinking planet." We are working in this direction in the Heifer Project. And we welcome every honest coop-

---

3. Hocking, 46.

erator. This includes churchless and stateless people too. [Arnold] Toynbee is optimistic here: "Our age will not be remembered for its horrifying crimes, or its astonishing inventions, but because it is the first age since the dawn of history in which mankind dared to believe it practicable to make the benefits of civilization available to the whole human race." All of this under God. Something like this could be a real beginning of a sound world government.

A rather homely illustration might be helpful here. Some years ago, after a very strenuous summer in western camps, I had the opportunity of doing a little fishing in the ocean. It was genuine fun to be a member of a good-natured group of forty persons dropping lines and hopefully holding poles over the side of a barge anchored five miles out from the shore. It was exciting to watch somebody else a few feet away pull up a fish from one hundred feet down. It was more exciting to pull in one yourself. But the real aim was to catch a yellowtail.

All at once my line grew taut. There was tension aplenty as my line was moved about in the water by something big on the other end. Of course, I held on and wound my reel. By an unwritten law everyone else on that side of the boat pulled his line back in to give me free room to land my fish. And advice came in from all sides. One bit of it I remember: "Hold her head up!" I was trying to do that, but my unskilled arms could not do it. As in a good many other fish stories, the big one got away, even before I got to see it. Maybe it *was* a yellowtail.

But the advice still holds. It is the church's job to hold the state's head up—on honesty, on religious liberty, and on world planning for human welfare.

As citizens, individual Brethren have something of a sliding scale of citizenship. In totalitarian states like Nazi Germany we might have slid to near zero. Some Mennonites still hold to that policy in other countries. But in some states the citizenship of Brethren might approach one hundred percent—more like that of some Friends. The more nearly the policy of the state approaches the mind of Christ, the fuller can be our citizenship. The farther it shifts away from the mind of Christ, the smaller our citizenship must become. But the tension must always be in the same direction, toward more responsibility to match our religious liberty—and to match our faith, whether we have religious liberty or not. This is part of what will help to transform the state someday.

We Brethren have a long way to go ourselves, but we have the task of doing more than our share to keep tension on the state toward Christian brotherhood as the highest form of order. In our changing world the possibilities for this are increasing along with the risks of the space age.

Let me summarize again:

1. Anarchy is *not* the highest form of order.

2. Obedience to the state is *not* the highest form of order.

3. National sovereignty is *not* the highest form of order.

4. To meet the intricate problems, Brethren will not run away in any sense; nor will we adjust to the state on any major problem. Further, we cannot allow any major splitting of personality. Instead, we will take on the Herculean task of transforming the state. But more than that, we will maintain a personal and group discipleship to our Master as our major responsibility. Then we shall have much to share with a needy state and a needy world toward Christian brotherhood—the highest form of order.

Somebody described the early Christians as "absolutely fearless, absurdly happy, and always in trouble." That does not yet describe us Brethren. Sometimes we miss it on all three counts. But as we build a group integrity appropriate to a Christian culture we shall become increasingly self-respecting and fearless. As we live closer to our Master we shall become happier deep down. And as we venture out beyond conventional practices we shall come into increasing tension with the modern state, with always enough trouble to keep life interesting and heroic. Can the modern state be transformed? All of them? There is no light answer, but "for the Christian to give the world up as lost is to give God up."[4]

It is the duty of the Brethren and all churches to keep at this unfinished task until "the kingdom of the world has become the kingdom of our Lord and of his Christ." This idea cannot be fully expressed without music. Handel's *Messiah* does it better. Brotherhood under the lordship of Christ is the highest goal for the Brethren and also for the modern state.

---

4. Hocking, 108.

VIII.

DUNKER IDENTITY

Always the skilled teacher and communicator, West loved drawing illustrations from common experiences and pairing them with lists of Brethren distinctives. In the first writing, a so-called "flower catalog," West proposed "pictures" of the Brethren way, which included suspicion of titles, respect for both the Bible and the findings of modern science, and rejection of anarchy. Fittingly, obedience to Christ and opposition to war are central to any Brethren identity.

The final two writings deal with peace and, more surprisingly for West, self-respect. In this poignant final essay, West returned to the 1920s and tells the story of how he came to personally affirm his Brethren heritage. He urged Brethren to accept and fulfill the best part of their heritage, and to transcend its limited perspectives. All traditions, West reminded the reader, can be improved upon. None have unquestioned allegiance or virtue.

The Brethren Flower Catalog

When we are at our best, we Brethren want many good things to become part of our way of living. Here are some of our targets on conduct; yes, we miss them often—and badly. Someday we hope to raise some "flowers" that will resemble the following sketches much more closely:

NB. These are some of the choice *pictures* from our "catalog."

1. We follow the commandments of Jesus, without being just literalists. What he says is to be done, even if it is hard. Here is one example: "Forgive—seventy times seven" [Matt. 18:22, RSV adapted]. We try not to dodge any of his will.

2. We stick up for justice and righteousness—and for love and mercy too. We oppose evil, but also oppose war methods against evil. We help the suffering on *both* sides of any struggle.

3. We hold steady to a pacifist faith, but do not coerce anybody's conscience. "No force in religion."

4. We keep on using the Bible (emphasizing the New Testament) and the microscope, telescope, and the spectroscope, and other research methods—everywhere we can.

5. We make the home central and the church, too—a difficult task. In both places we seek the "fellowship of kindred minds," even when we disagree.

6. We respect personality and yet use first names and nicknames. We do not respect titles or money or position or age. Brotherhood has no "levels."

7. Everybody should bear his own burden—as far as he can. But we bear one another's burdens, where help is needed. We help people to help themselves.

8. We must have order. Instead of chaos we would choose a dictatorship, but that is not the right kind of order for us. We are outgrowing *Robert's Rules of Order*, toward more brotherly rules.

Dan West, August 1955, box 50, Dan West Papers, Brethren Historical Library and Archives.

9. We like [Alexander] Hamilton's political philosophy and [Thomas] Jefferson's too. We hold together in Annual Conference, but keep a lot of freedom in local churches.

10. We carry on the essential rural values (taking responsibility, planning far ahead, finishing the job) even when we go into big cities.

11. We do much with little.

12. We work with anybody "going our way." But we prefer the "little people." E.g., Nathan Leopold; also resettling distressed Negro families.

13. Our deeds and our words fit together—a necessary factor in integrity.

14. Our service must not be detached from our testimony or our worship—integrity again.

15. We are optimistic in a pessimistic world. We believe in Christian brotherhood *and* world brotherhood in a world of bitter struggle.

16. We are dependable—yet unpredictable. "A Dunker's word is as good as his note." Also—"You can't tell what they will do next—but it will be something good."

17. _____

18. _____

19. _____

Brethren Ideals—Peace

"God is love" [1 John 4:8]. This central teaching of the New Testament is an emphasis for Brethren and for other historic peace groups. And we hold that Jesus' teachings are not to be explained away, but to be taken about as they are given.

The big, confused, floundering world is a new thing for Brethren; only half a century ago we were detached from it. But now the pressures on all Christians are so heavy that the world cannot be ignored. And the glaring evils in it (including Russian philosophy and methods) cannot be explained away either. God is righteousness, also, as the Old Testament teaches. Those people who emphasize that part of the Bible lean heavily toward punishment, even to destroying other people for the evil they have done.

Here comes the hard problem—to love evildoers or to punish them? With small children it may be possible to both love and punish, but with grown-ups, or with groups of them, it may not be possible. With nations it is impossible. With Edmund Burke we must agree: "You cannot indict a nation." Sometimes a very important choice must be made: Shall we stand for righteousness or for love?

The usual answer to this is clear: Punish first, never mind the love until afterward. Psychologists have an explanation for this attitude—the self-righteousness of the self-appointed "policeman." Many Christians have even enjoyed hating and killing. But this is a long way from believing that "God is love."

In recent years, however, consciences have been growing. A surprising number of people without our background are looking at this peace doctrine, and are beginning to understand it. War is always wrong: "There is no Christian way to kill a man," or an army of them, or a cityful of men, women, and children—no matter how evil someone else has been.

But many people are unable to break away from the war system, even though they know it is wrong. Some have tried to rationalize it, and "kill repentantly." In 1918 an eminent divine, praying for *our* soldiers, asked that they might "kill in the spirit of love." Such nonsense cannot long exist in an honest Christian; better to choose the killing and make the most of it, or else choose Christ's way at all costs.

Dan West, December 22, 1950, box 50, Dan West Papers, Brethren Historical Library and Archives.

Here Brethren must be very humble—we have not done too well. But the ideal has been steady, thank God. Also, it belongs to the Brethren genius that our ideals have first claim on our actions. NOW more than ever before is the time to put our ideals into our practice.

Someday the world will come to see that Jesus' way is the only practical way of life. But it must be demonstrated first. If Brethren count the cost first and then decide to pay more than their share of it—take up the cross daily—the world will be redeemed sooner, maybe soon enough to prevent another world war.

Self-Respecting Dunkers*

A small boy had the weekly task of carrying butter and eggs from the farm home to several families in a little village a long mile away. Of course he walked and usually along or on the railroad tracks. Out of this extended experience he made some new friends and learned more about buying and selling and other things. These people were different and some were superior to him—so he felt. Other villagers were "better" also, especially some from other church groups. His own Dunker folks were likeable enough (part of the time), but they could not measure up so well. They were just good to bring in butter and eggs.

Long years afterward he read in an unusual book, *Resolving Social Conflicts*, a strange chapter with the title, "Self-Hatred among Jews." The author was Kurt Lewin, a Jewish psychologist who had left Germany in time for his own safety. His deep insight into many matters is still growing in influence. In that chapter almost as in a mirror I saw myself as I had felt as a small boy and youth—of course the dates and names were changed. The meaning, however, was crystal clear: I had hated the culture which had helped to produce me (some call it a "subculture"). This was a surprising discovery.

Many other Dunkers have felt this way and some still feel it, especially youth where cultural ways are changing rapidly. If these handicapped youth and older people can be helped to outgrow these feelings of inferiority based on cultural differences, they can build a healthier self-respect. With such help in my youth I could have had a better meaning to life during those years—and maybe since, too.

Back in the 1920s, a year at Cornell University gave me a new chance to learn new people and ideas and cultural meanings. During that Christmas vacation back home I spent a weekend at a youth conference in Southern Ohio. Sure, these folks were green, with plenty of lacks and faults—I knew them well enough. But in that short time I came to feel, "This is my bunch."

*A Spanish psychologist who had never heard of us became much interested in us. As I outlined a bit, he observed that I had used our real name, Church of the Brethren, and our nickname, "Dunkers." When I interpreted he smiled and suggested, "You had better call yourselves 'Dunkers' until you really are Brethren."

Dan West, "Self-Respecting Dunkers," *Brethren Life and Thought*, vol. 10, Spring 1965, 44-46.

That new feeling lasted all through the rest of that year; and it has grown since then. With it came a better appreciation for people from other cultures. My own self-respect and respect for them deepened together.

Beyond these personal meanings I can understand better the constructive values of any culture which helps to produce anybody of basic worth—and that includes all of us. Certainly some cultures are better than others. All are mixed—with some good elements and plenty of others. And none is good enough. We need a better understanding of the truth about cultures and how we look at them. Here is an eloquent meaning from a Jewish subculture in czarist Russia. "How do we keep our balance? I can tell you in one word—tradition. Because of our traditions everyone here knows who he is and what God expects him to do" (from *Fiddler on the Roof*).

Self-hatred, whether conscious or not, makes people feel confused and less than worthy—often far below what is justified. Their assets are downgraded because others' are somehow "better." They are rated higher than is justifiable—often much higher. This feeling may account for much of cultural change—the "upward mobility" of modern America, for one example. Status becomes very important. Advertisers can play on inferiority feelings to their own economic advantages. The "Joneses" are always better than we are, and so we must try to keep up with them. Promoters can thus make us want to eat and drink as the Joneses do, smoke as they smoke, dress and talk and act like them, have cars and furnishings like theirs, build churches and plan worship services like theirs, have schools and colleges and curricula like theirs—and even theologies—all "superior" to ours (so we feel). Thus good people can become part of the aimless, lonely crowd, where nobody has any dependable culture, largely because everybody hates the culture in which he grew up.

After the ancient Hebrew people lost their cultural self-respect, they wanted "a king like other nations." Well, they got him: first Saul, who later went to pieces; then David the warrior and empire builder, also the adulterer and psalmist; then Solomon, who lived it up. After him "the deluge" with degeneration and disintegration and chaos—except for a little remnant who held on to some basic elements of their old culture. A few centuries ago in England a little handful of "different" people, very methodical about many things, were contemptuously called "Methodists." Earlier another handful were called "Quakers" because they tried to "work out their own salvation with fear and trembling." Earlier yet some others in Europe were called "Protestants"—and not with any real respect. Centuries before that in Antioch in Syria some "queer" people were called "Christians" by their critics. The meanings of these terms of contempt have changed for the better since. In some places the term *Dunker* has improved also; e.g., "A Dunker's word is as good as his note."

Not many years ago I had a chance to meet persons from many different cultures. And in every culture I learned about were some good things and some not so good—just as in mine. Some persons hated their culture and were anxious to take on another—of course that new one was "better." But some of these people respected their own culture. I warmed up to them much more, even when I could not agree with them.

It is more fun to think with self-respecting Germans and Spaniards, Greeks and Turks, Persians and Indians, Koreans and Japanese than with people who hate their culture. Also it is much more rewarding to meet self-respecting Jews, Muslims, Hindus, Parsees, and Buddhists than self-hating Christians, of whatever denomination. Differences? Yes, plenty of them; and some differences are very important.

It is easier to work with people with a cultural self-respect. This is similar to working with people with a personal self-respect. It is a great gain to come to respect one's own culture and that of others at the same time. They usually develop together. Here is the best formula I know for people who want to hold steady as they try to live well in a rapidly changing world:

1. Accept your early culture. It could not have been all bad, since it helped produce you. If you accept it as *wholly* good, however, you are likely ignorant or dishonest. But if you just can't see anything good in it, you are likely blinded by self-hatred.

2. Fulfill the best part of it. When working in the attic, we need to sort out the junk; but it is worth the effort. Maybe some real heirlooms will be discovered with the junk. NB. It takes an alert and discerning person always to label things correctly. Better not call junk "heirlooms" or heirlooms "junk." It is right to be honest and reasonably accurate.

3. Transcend it—like a husky little plant breaking up through the hard ground. Nobody's culture is good enough—really adequate for responsible Christian living in the modern world. We need to create a new culture, borrowing the best from every older culture, including our own.

INDEX OF NAMES

O
Oppenheimer, J. Robert, 119
Orr, John Boyd, 139

P
Palmer, E. L., 28
Pierlot, Hubert, 70

Q
Quinter, James, 28

R
Rankin, Jeannette, 32, 111
Rauschenbusch, Walter, 6
Reich, John, 66
Richards, Fred, 84
Richards, Ned, 116
Rogers, Will, 111
Rohrer, Perry, 3
Roling, Bert, 41
Roop, Roger, 71, 72
Roosevelt, Franklin, 31, 109
Roosevelt, Theodore, 136
Row, Harold, 4
Rupel, Martha, 65

S
Sauer, Christopher, 142
Schweitzer, Albert, 52
Shaffer, Ken, ix
Shamberger, Chauncey, 3
Shawcross, Hartley, 105, 144
Slabaugh, W. W., 144
Smuts, Jan, 105, 144
Snow, C. P., 33
Socrates, 42
Steigerwalt, A. K., 48
Stevenson, Robert Louis, 109

Stine, O. W., 69
Stresemann, Gustav, 31
Swigart, William J., 9, 11

T
Tennyson, Alfred, 22, 117
Tillich, Paul, 5, 129, 134
Toynbee, Arnold, 147
Truman, Harry, 30, 89

V
Van Dyke, Joe, 3, 9, 22

W
Weir, Samuel, ix, 2
Wells, H. G., 32
West, Barbara Landis, 2, 9, 12-13
West, Landon, ix, 2, 12
West, Lucy Sherck, 3, 61, 63-64
West, P. C., 27

Z
Zigler, M. R., 66

INDEX OF SCRIPTURES

All scripture quotations are from the Revised Standard Version of the Bible (RSV), unless otherwise noted. Other translations used include:

- *KJV—King James Version*
- *NET—New English Translation*

OLD TESTAMENT

Leviticus
25:10, 136

Esther
4:14, 135

Psalms
51:5, 95
122:6, 105

Proverbs
22:6, 113
30:8*b*-9, 50

Isaiah
55:11, 95

NEW TESTAMENT

Matthew
5:6, 111
5:48, 80
6:11, 67, 115
7:21, 24, 40
13:22, 48
18:22, 151
23, 99
26:41, 95

Luke
12:15, 45, 50

John
8:32, 87, 122
14:12, 135
14:15, 40

Acts
17:24, 42